Archetypal Ontology

In this novel re-examination of the archetype construct, philosopher Jon Mills and psychiatrist Erik Goodwyn engage in spirited dialogue on the origins, nature, and scope of what archetypes actually constitute, their relation to the greater questions of psyche and worldhood, and their relevance for Jungian studies and analytical psychology today.

Arguably the most definitive feature of Jung's metapsychology is his theory of archetypes. It is the fulcrum on which his analytical depth psychology rests. With recent trends in post-Jungian and neo-Jungian perspectives that have embraced developmental, relational, social justice, and postmodern paradigms, classical archetype theory has largely become a drowning genre. Despite the archetypal school of James Hillman and his contemporaries, and the archetype debates that captured our attention over two decades ago, contemporary Jungians are preoccupied with the lived reality of the existential subject and the personal unconscious over the collective transpersonal forces derived from archaic ontology.

Archetypal Ontology will be of interest to psychoanalysts, philosophers, transpersonal psychologists, cultural theorists, anthropologists, religious scholars, and scholars of many disciplines in the arts and humanities, analytical psychology, and post-Jungian studies.

Jon Mills, PsyD, PhD, ABPP, is a Canadian philosopher and psychoanalyst. He is Honorary Professor at the Department of Psychosocial & Psychoanalytic Studies, University of Essex, UK, as well as a faculty member in the postgraduate programs in psychoanalysis and psychotherapy at the Gordon F. Derner School of Psychology, Adelphi University, and the New School for Existential Psychoanalysis, USA. He is the recipient of numerous awards for his scholarship, and the author and/or editor of over 30 books in philosophy, psychoanalysis, and cultural studies.

Erik Goodwyn, MD, is Clinical Associate Professor, Department of Psychiatry, WWAMI University of Washington School of Medicine-Billings, Montana affiliate. He has authored numerous publications in the field of consciousness studies, Jungian psychology, neuroscience, mythology, philosophy, anthropology, and the psychology of religion, including 5 books. He is co-Editor-in-Chief of the *International Journal of Jungian Studies.*

Philosophy & Psychoanalysis Book Series
Jon Mills
Series Editor

Philosophy & Psychoanalysis is dedicated to current developments and cutting-edge research in the philosophical sciences, phenomenology, hermeneutics, existentialism, logic, semiotics, cultural studies, social criticism, and the humanities that engage and enrich psychoanalytic thought through philosophical rigor. With the philosophical turn in psychoanalysis comes a new era of theoretical research that revisits past paradigms while invigorating new approaches to theoretical, historical, contemporary, and applied psychoanalysis. No subject or discipline is immune from psychoanalytic reflection within a philosophical context including psychology, sociology, anthropology, politics, the arts, religion, science, culture, physics, and the nature of morality. Philosophical approaches to psychoanalysis may stimulate new areas of knowledge that have conceptual and applied value beyond the consulting room reflective of greater society at large. In the spirit of pluralism, *Philosophy & Psychoanalysis* is open to any theoretical school in philosophy and psychoanalysis that offers novel, scholarly, and important insights in the way we come to understand our world.

Titles in this series:

Enriching Psychoanalysis
Integrating Concepts from Contemporary Science and Philosophy
Edited by John Turtz and Gerald J. Gargiulo

Psyche, Culture, World
Excursions in Existentialism and Psychoanalytic Philosophy
by Jon Mills

The Emergent Container in Psychoanalysis
Experiencing Absence and Future
by Ana Martinez Acobi

Archetypal Ontology
New Directions in Analytical Psychology
by Jon Mills and Erik Goodwyn

Archetypal Ontology

New Directions in Analytical Psychology

Jon Mills and Erik Goodwyn

Routledge
Taylor & Francis Group

LONDON AND NEW YORK

Designed cover image: Fishing by Levitation by
Bob 'Omar' Tunnoch, www.bobomartunnoch.com

First published 2023
by Routledge
4 Park Square, Milton Park, Abingdon, Oxon OX14 4RN

and by Routledge
605 Third Avenue, New York, NY 10158

Routledge is an imprint of the Taylor & Francis Group, an informa business

British Library Cataloguing-in-Publication Data
A catalogue record for this book is available from the British Library

ISBN: 978-1-032-39481-7 (hbk)
ISBN: 978-1-032-39480-0 (pbk)
ISBN: 978-1-003-34992-1 (ebk)

DOI: 10.4324/9781003349921

Typeset in Times New Roman
by codeMantra

Contents

Prolegomenon   viii
JON MILLS

1   The essence of archetypes   1
    JON MILLS

2   Archetypal origins: Biology vs culture is a false dichotomy   28
    ERIK GOODWYN

3   On the origins of archetypes   45
    JON MILLS

4   Commentary on Mills' "The essence of archetypes"   50
    ERIK GOODWYN

5   Archetypal metaphysics and the psyworld   59
    JON MILLS

6   The origins of psyche: From experience to ontology   77
    ERIK GOODWYN

7   Archetype, psyche, world: From experience to cosmopsychism   95
    JON MILLS

8   Psyche, world, archetype: Final thoughts   113
    ERIK GOODWYN

About the authors   135
Index   137

Prolegomenon

Jon Mills

Arguably, the most definitive feature of Jung's metapsychology is his theory of archetypes. It is the fulcrum on which his analytical depth psychology rests. With recent trends in post-Jungian and neo-Jungian perspectives that have embraced evolutionary science, attachment theory, developmental, relational, and postmodern paradigms, as well as social justice activism, classical archetype theory has largely become a drowning genre. Despite the archetypal school of James Hillman and his contemporaries and the Cambridge archetype debates that captured our attention over two decades ago, contemporary Jungians are preoccupied with the lived reality of the existential subject and the personal unconscious over the collective transpersonal forces derived from archaic ontology. In our re-examination of the archetype construct, Erik Goodwyn and I engage in spirited dialogue on the origins, nature, and scope of what archetypes actually constitute, their relation to the greater questions of psyche and worldhood, and their relevance for Jungian studies and analytical psychology today.

Apart from offering a novel theory of mind and cosmos, what is unique about this book is the structure, format, style, and approach to mutual critique. Each of us presents a chapter on the essence and origins of archetypes, only then to critique each other's work in an ongoing interchange of ideas, challenges, and joint criticisms where both agreements and disagreements are fleshed out from different vantage points in the human sciences. This dialogical format builds on each other's previous theses and arguments, clarifies ambiguities, and refines earlier theoretical commitments that naturally develop into more fruitful comparisons in methodology and content that are mutually compatible and complementary in focus. As the discussion unfolds in an organic fashion, we move beyond the parameters of archetype theory to engage the greater questions of what constitutes psyche, world, and a transpersonal collective mind. The end result leads us to entertain a psychic cosmogony based in speculative metaphysics that offers new perspectives in ontology, which further expands and enriches Jung's original theory of a collective unconscious.

To this day, there is no unified consensus on what constitutes an archetype. Even Jung himself was murky at best. Jungians are divided and propose contradictory—if not unintelligible theories—about the ground, breadth, and limits to archetypal discourse, ranging from uncritical acceptance of classical paradigms to dismissing the notion altogether. This book provides a corrective in clarity and debate between two scholars from two different backgrounds: one from philosophy and psychoanalysis, the other from the biological sciences and psychiatry. Together these dialogues are unique in the history of Jungian psychology for they approach the archetype question from sundry points of view including metaphysics, onto-phenomenology, philosophy of mind, evolutionary biology, neuroscience, and cultural anthropology. Taken as a whole, we suggest, these exchanges advance the discipline of analytical psychology with philosophical, scientific, and logical rigor. The result is a new theory of archetypes and psyche that are deconstructed from their historical origins, updated, and theoretically refined to account for conventions in understanding the interface between philosophy, psychology, bioscience, and culture in modern society today.

Overview and new directions

Jung's notion of the archetype remains an equivocal concept, so much so that Jungians and post-Jungians have failed to agree on its essential nature. In Chapter 1, I wish to argue that an archetype may be understood as an unconscious schema that is self-constitutive and emerges into consciousness from its own a priori ground, hence an autonomous self-determinative act derived from archaic ontology. After offering an analysis of the archetype debate, I set out to philosophically investigate the essence of an archetype by examining its origins and dialectical reflections as a process system arising from its own autochthonous parameters. I offer a descriptive explication of the inner constitution and birth of an archetype based on internal rupture and the desire to project its universality, form, and patternings into psychic reality as self-instantiating replicators. Archetypal content is the appearance of essence as the products of self-manifestation, for an archetype must appear in order to be made actual. Here we must seriously question that, in the beginning, if an archetype is self-constituted and self-generative, the notion and validity of a collective unconscious become rather dubious, if not superfluous. I conclude by sketching out an archetypal theory of alterity based on dialectical logic.

In Chapter 2, Erik Goodwyn offers his thesis on archetypal origins and argues that the framing of the debate as being either derived from biology versus culture is a false dichotomy. Here, he argues that the question of whether or not archetypes are transmitted biologically or culturally is wrongly posed and has hampered progress in Jungian thought regarding archetype theory. Considerations regarding psychological development show that some contents of the human psyche are, strictly speaking, neither biologically nor culturally derived. Various examples are given that question and affect the nature of archetype theory, which he examines in depth.

In response to his chapter, I readdress the question and origins of archetypes in this ongoing debate that has historically focused on privileging one causal factor over another and argue that Goodwyn offers a mesotheory of archetypal origins that displaces the radical bifurcation of either biology or culture as primary categories. I offer my own reflections on the origins of archetypes and argue that this discussion can be further advanced by addressing the question of unconscious agency.

In turn, Goodwyn offers a commentary on my chapter on the essence of archetypes where I examine archetypal process merely in terms of what must occur for archetypal content to emerge in consciousness, without reference to neuroscience or biology, but rather on a purely experiential level. Goodwyn rightly notes how I seek to understand what essential characteristics the archetype-as-such must have in order to give rise to archetypal experiences, focusing on how I remain entirely within the intrapsychic realm so as not to muddy the waters with any discussion of first substance, which I feel is epistemologically messy. Goodwyn critiques this maneuver for its merits and weakness, yet still providing a new set of conceptual tools with which to understand the archetype in terms of its internal constellations, dynamics, and consistent qualities. In so doing, Goodwyn also questions my failure to engage in any discussion about what (if any) biological or other contributions there may be to the archetype. He believes this creates a discourse that has a certain purity and precision to it by showing in a powerful and logical way how such concerns are actually unnecessary to demonstrate the necessity of the concept of archetype no matter what sort of metaphysics one employs. But regardless of this strength in my approach, a method I refer to as onto-phenomenology, the fact remains that we humans are enmattered beings, and the matter of which we are composed (or equivalent to, or otherwise, depending on your metaphysics) has certain regularities to it as given to us by the observations of the biological sciences. So, my refusal to engage with this question as such, he argues, will only give us a partial answer to the question of archetypal origins. That said, he remains unconvinced, at least on this point, that we can fully discuss archetypal origins without some kind of metaphysics of mind lurking in the background, even if it is not specifically stated, or, as I do in my chapter, deliberately avoid. It is at this stage in our dialogue that we pick up on the metaphysical parameters of an archetype and the psyche itself.

As a rejoinder to his commentary, in Chapter 5 I address Professor Goodwyn's insightful and nuanced critique of my work on the essence of archetypes that have direct bearing on his own investigations of archetypal origins, attractor states, the mind-body problem, and on the question of metaphysics. Goodwyn's work is grounded in scientific naturalism while I offer an onto-phenomenological methodology that is compatible with his own positions. The questions of embodiment, ground, holism, panpsychism, and *esse in anima* are examined in light of offering a preliminary framework for an archetypal metaphysics where I introduce a theory of *psyworld*.

In Chapter 6, Goodwyn critiques my theory of psyworld. Because our challenge is expanding from the certainty of individual experience into the metaphysical beyond of a more large-scale ontological framework, his chapter attempts to do just that. In doing so, he tries to bridge the theoretical gap between our respective methodologies by answering to my call for action starting from onto-phenomenology and then seeing if we can progress logically from there to wind up at the position Goodwyn starts with, namely, *cosmopsychism*. Here he tries to situate the archetype in a way that is consilient with both of our conceptual approaches.

In our dialogues thus far over the nature of archetypes, essence, psyche, and world, I further respond to Professor Goodwyn's foray into establishing an ontological position that not only answers to the mind-body problem, but further locates the source of Psyche on a cosmic plane. His impressive attempt to launch a neo-Jungian metaphysics is based on the principle of cosmic panpsychism that bridges both the internal parameters of archetypal process and their emergence in consciousness and the external world conditioned by a psychic universe. Here, I explore the ontology of experience, mind, matter, and metaphysical realism, and I critique Goodwyn's turn to Neoplatonism. The result is a potentially compatible theory of mind and reality that grounds archetypal theory in onto-phenomenology, metaphysics, and bioscience, hence facilitating new, redirecting conceptual shifts in analytical psychology.

In the last chapter, Goodwyn offers his final reflections on our discussions and attempts to clarify the biggest differences between our positions on the subject of psyche and world. My critique of his application of holistic cosmopsychism to Jungian psychology highlighted several areas that needed clarification. Toward that end, he provides a clearer description of where our approaches intersect.

Aporias

In summarizing our methodological differences, my investigation of archetype, psyche, and world remains within the realm of the human being while Goodwyn attributes psyche to the cosmos itself that thereby conditions the human mind and all experience. While I bracket such ontological commitments, Goodwyn uses logical abduction to infer a first principle that is derived from the universe as a whole, hence psyche is presupposed in the basic elements that constitute matter. Despite complementarity and compatibility, I believe our differences hinge on the hermeneutics, functions, and semiotics of what we mean by "consciousness," which naturally brings forth its own set of semantic, ontological, and epistemological delimitations that do not necessarily require resolve for us to appreciate how psyche and world are ontically constituted through the metaphysics of holistic experience.

One remaining conundrum to any attempt to explain origins, as we both endeavor to do, is that we are up against the problem of infinite regression. Appealing to a brute foundationalism, ground, or precondition that conditions all conditions leads us to bump up against the question and (un) answerability of the *original point* origins, which we must perennially question, if not simply acquiesce to ignorance or aporetic ineffability. This is no different in physics as it is in metaphysics, as we still must appeal to original conditions that serve as an *explanans* to an *explanandum*. And how do we finagle our way through reason to a pre-original cause when all we observe and experience are appearances? For example, how do we explain how the universe as a whole got here to begin with, let alone how it was endowed with consciousness? Was it acquired or simply given as brute occurrence? In other words, we can't begin to answer what the *pre-original event* or *pre-origins of origins* are, let alone how the universe as a whole already possesses consciousness as its essential nature, which is required to explain the division and dispersal of its essence into the human mind.

If the cosmos is causal, conditions, and brings about human consciousness, then what conditions the structure of cosmic consciousness? We would need to appeal to how the universe came into being as a whole, unless we rely on a theory of brute thrownness *or* emergence, that it is derived from a previous consciousness (which we would still need to explain) that causes the cosmic whole, or that it was always present—an infinity that is self-constituted. Is this not simply another word for God? Or perhaps a collective unconscious that conditions, saturates, and sustains the universe? No wonder why Jung posited that God was unconscious. Regardless of the mystical and apophantic dimensions to our meandering yet focused discussion, we hope the reader will appreciate how classical archetype theory not only becomes resuscitated from its impending death in contemporary Jungian discourse, but rather opens new vistas for depth psychology informed by a robust metaphysics.

Chapter 1

The essence of archetypes

Jon Mills

What constitutes the essence of an archetype? In other words, what makes it what it truly is, *exactly*, without which it would not be? Jung failed to make this clear. And post-Jungian schools including contemporary Jungian movements have still not answered this most elemental question. As a result, there is no clarity or consensus among the profession. The term "archetype" is thrown about and employed, I suggest, without proper understanding or analysis of its essential features. This essay aims to provide a possible corrective to such theoretical ambiguities and *aporias* in order to rehabilitate the definition, clarity, and value this term properly conveys. Here, any exposition of an archetype must stand in relation to the question of origins.

Archetypal theory must contend with the inner parameters of what constitutes an archetype's essence, scope, and ground for appearance. As such, I will offer a dialectical account of the inner constitution of an archetype with an emphasis on the ontology of difference as a pivotal feature. I propose that the internal configuration of an archetype entails its own dialectical relations and tensions to otherness *within* its own constitution, which becomes the template for external differentiation, projection, and self-manifestation revealed through alterity. What I have in mind is exploring to what degree otherness is not only ontologically necessary for identity, but is also the instantiation of internal division that becomes unfamiliar and alienated from the internal fabric of an archetype itself, hence giving rise to modified forms as the differentiation of its original essence. What this means is that all instantiations of archetypal process originally arise from their own internal division as a dialectical mediation to otherness that becomes externalized through specific forms and particularities. In what follows, I hope to articulate the metaphysical factors and internal operations of the activities of an archetype that enrich a theoretic justification for postulating an original ground and grounding for archaic ontology to manifest and re-inscribe itself through archetypal phenomena. Put laconically, I will attempt to elucidate a new theory of archetypes based on the dynamics of internal rupture, division, and exteriorization manifesting as unconscious schemata.

DOI: 10.4324/9781003349921-1

The archetype debate

The field of Jungian studies cannot agree upon what constitutes Jung's most original contributions to psychological theory, namely, the doctrine of archetypes. Nowhere, that is, in no other psychoanalytic tradition, I suggest, do we witness such a debate where the most fundamental aspect of a community's theoretical framework is challenged. The *most basic theoretical tenet* of the founding father of the movement is repeatedly drawn into question within post-classical, reformed, and contemporary perspectives to the degree that there is no unified consensus on what defines or constitutes an archetype. This opens up the field to criticism—to being labeled an esoteric scholarly specialty, insular self-interest group, or Gnostic guild, even a mystic cult, unfairly I might add. Jungianism needs to rehabilitate its image, arguably to modernize its appeal to other academic and clinical disciplines and make it attractive to the masses. Here, I concur with many others, its allure and success is in addressing the question of the spiritual (Mills, 2017), a shortcoming of traditional psychoanalysis. But the ontology of the archetype, although repeatedly denied by Jung's followers and apologists as making no metaphysical claims whatsoever, lies at the very heart of this conundrum. What is missing is a proper *philosophical* expatiation and analysis of the essence of archetypes, a theoretical scaffolding I hope to remediate in what follows.

Let us briefly begin with Jung, who had referred to the archetypes in so many varied, convoluted, and contradictory ways, that his conjectural legacy was bound to be taken up by post-Jungian and contemporary scholars in an effort to expound, de-convolute, and clean up the theoretical mess. Jung referred to archetypes as inborn ideas, forms, collective images, instincts, affective organizations, fantasies, emotions, behavioral patterns, and qualitative intensities such as numinosity (*CW*, 8: pp. 133, 195, 201, 205–206, 436; Jung, 1957, p. xliv; 1964, p. 96). In other places in the *Collected Works*, he calls them psychic energies, entities, and independent forces and agencies that are autonomously organized and can seize or impose themselves on a person against their own volition (*CW*, 8; p. 231; Jung 1961, p. 347). Furthermore, he attributes mind-independence to archetypes, which have a transcendental character, and that they exist outside of naturalized accounts of space and time due to their supernatural structure and presence (*CW*, 14: pp. 505, 536–538, 551–552; also averred in his interview with Freeman, 1959). But Jung also referred to archetypes as concepts, hypotheses, heuristic models, and metaphors (*CW*, 9, p. 160) when he was backtracking from his earlier philosophic commitments under the banner of science. And he was very clear to announce that he was conducting empirical psychology, not speculative philosophy, and went to great lengths to claim that his theories had nothing to do with metaphysics (*CW*, 11: p. 16) despite the fact that he was engaging ontology. This is not a convincing, let alone coherent or sustainable, argument. So, where does this leave us?

May I suggest that the controversy over the fate of the archetype concept has traditionally been framed in the following binary categories, if not false dichotomies: (1) *The Rationalism vs. Empiricism debate*, which engages the general questions of a priorism versus experience; (2) *The Biology vs. Culture debate*, which engages the more specific questions of innateness, evolution, and genetic transmission versus the role of the environment, attachment, developmental psychology, language, and social dynamics; and (3) *The Naturalism vs. Supernaturalism debate*, which engages and intersects the previous categories with many micro-debates that situate nuanced arguments within naturalized embodied paradigms within complex social structures versus transpersonal, transubjective, suprapersonal, transcendent entities, agencies, and energies that have supernatural foundations, organizations, and mystical properties, which evoke greater metaphysical questions such as emanationism, supervenience, and the God posit.

The question of a priorism or innateness can be approached from both rationalist philosophical traditions as well as empirical ones, whether that be from speculative metaphysics with an emphasis on first principles, to propositional logic, and the grounding and function of our epistemological processes including logical positivism, to the role of biology, evolution, genetics, cognition, neuroscience, epigenetics, attachment theory, developmental and social psychology, and the nature of universals. Developmentalists quarrel with evolutionary biologists, and environmentalists or sociologists abhor any reductive paradigms that boil an archetype down to its substantive (materially) deterministic nature, even if it is an a priori ontological condition for subsequent human development. And both naturalists and culturalists object to the theosophic implications of importing onto-theology into any discussion of the constitution of an archetype. Please forgive me if I am being too simplistic here, but there seems to be four predominant groups that overlap and debate: (1) evolutionists, (2) developmentalists, (3) culturalists, and (4) transpersonalists, followed by a series of supple disputes within each camp that may annex other perspectives, such as developmental emergentism, and hence highlights the complexity of archetype theory.

Erik Goodwyn (2010) reconsiders the question of innateness and the argument from inheritance, which he juxtaposes to current trends that view archetypes as a confluence of developmental and constructivist processes that become dynamic emergent systems and properties (Hogenson, 2001; Saunders & Skar, 2001), such as image schemas (Knox, 2003). The locus of this nuanced deliberation is on how much do we inherit from evolutionary pressures and genetic conditioning versus how developmental-psychosocial processes emerge within a socio-symbolic order that conditions the content of our psychic productions, which are not originally inherited. Stevens (2002) champions the classical biological approach, which more or less subsumes the cognitive and neurosciences, including the notion of brain-specific algorithms that are pre-programmed, pre-existent, and pre-specified, while developmentalists argue that anything symbolically meaningful cannot be inherited but only emerge from attachments and socialization processes within a cultural milieu. A priorists and evolutionists—from Kant to Darwin, are generically in agreement that basic constitutional predispositions condition all experience, while emergent theorists or dynamic systems models would emphasize the organizing power of experience over reductive causal forces, even if they were to concede that they still emerge from a corporeal a priori ground and become dynamically organized through complex interactions between genes, epigeneticity, and the environment, whether that be biologically embodied, socio-culturally mediated, or both. Of course, any discussion that privileges one side over the other, e.g., genetics versus culture, must contend with the thorny issues of causal determinism, personal freedom, choice, and agency, a debate we do not need to entertain here (see Mills, 2013b for a review).

Stevens (2002) goes so far to proclaim that, "When I define archetype as 'innate neuropsychic potential', I am talking about the *archetype-as-such*" (p. 284, italics in original). Here, he is referring to the *Ding an sich*, which is reduced to its ontological biological substrate. Following Jung's (and Freud's) Kantian affinities that the thing-in-itself cannot be directly known, only its derivatives, that is, we may only have epistemological access to the forms in which they appear, the paradigmatic example being *imago*, this type of dogmatic reductionism poses severe philosophical challenges. Boiling down archetypes to the brain is a crass biological realism that Raya Jones (2000) has referred to as a "myth of modernity" (p. 600). To say that the "real" archetype is a neurological correlate and property of the brain that causes emergence *as such* is to displace the rich discourse on the variegated modes of appearance and the phenomenology of lived experience that may be overdetermined and derived from multiple competing strands of causation and their subsequent meta-organizations and functions. Biology is a necessary condition of all psychological phenomena, but it is hardly a sufficient condition to explain the complexifications of mind and society. We can observe brain states in a fMRI or a CAT scan, for example, but these observations are not witnessing or recording consciousness. Consciousness is not colorful images on a computer screen. This is a mereological error, as well as the fallacy of simple location as misplaced concreteness. Consciousness cannot be collapsed into any physicalist paradigm without suffering the loss of soul. Psyche is much more than what these reductive models can proclaim, even if scientifically savvy and politically in vogue.

Back to the cultural wars, Christian Roesler (2012), like Jean Knox (2003), thinks that archetypes are transmitted more through social processes than biology, for complex symbolic patterns cannot be genetically encoded or inherited and should be conceived as originating from socialization. Hybrid determinist positions have also focused on the essence of archetypes from within the psyche and society, some solely from the standpoint of imagination (Hillman, 2013), as symbolic forms (Pietikainen, 1998), action patterns (Hogenson, 2009), as well as phenomenologically emergent from embodied human engagement and action in their social and physical environments within their linguistic world (Colman, 2016); while evolutionary proponents wish to argue for how biology is the basis for developmental, social, and cultural achievement despite being ontologically intertwined. Following those who have constructed empirical studies to provide so-called scientific "proof" for the existence of archetypes (see Maloney, 1999), Goodwyn (2013) argues that recurrent motifs in all societies function as "resonant attractors" that can be empirically studied in the narrative field and offers evidence for the existence of innate archetypes, although attractor positions could just as easily be explained through psychodynamic motivations based in unconscious desire, defense, and identification, so the micro-tensions between evolutionary psychology, developmental emergence, and sociological-cultural influence become a matter of emphasis, if not a moot point, not to mention the perils of proving epistemological validity.

Jung's introduction of the archetype as a transpersonal reality with transcendental properties that infiltrate and occupy the psyche of all people in all cultures but is unknowable in itself is often interpreted by those unsympathetic to this view as a magical construct from a supernatural provenance (see Jung, *CW*, 7, p. 187; *CW*, 8, p. 183, 209; *CW*, 9, p. 33). How could an archetype be floating about in space (yet is outside of spacetime but supervenes on the spatiotemporal mind) as an independent entity and agency that impregnates the psyche of all people, acts autonomously, seizes mental functioning, compels a person or social forces to act against their will, and claim that it is anchored in an archaic unconscious participatory process that is equated with and/or originates from God (see Jung, *CW*, 11, pp. 468–470)? Jung goes so far as to make an archetype a "living subject" (*CW*, 11, p. 469), a divine "arranger of psychic forms inside and outside the psyche" (see *Letters II*, p. 22).

It goes without saying that the naturalists would dismiss any supernatural claims as being unscientific, unverifiable, unfalsifiable, and bogus illusions, while the transpersonalists would question the epistemological arrogance of science, separate the categories of subjectivity, intersubjectivity, and objectivity as distinct modes of experience, being, and knowledge, reframe the realism versus idealism debate, expand the notion of what constitutes the parameters of naturalism, and favor a phenomenological and hermeneutic discourse over the empirical method. The objections to naturalism are often motivated by the need to preserve the notions of spirituality, theology, transcendence, and phenomenological or mystical experience, when naturalists and logical positivists oppose such phenomena based on ideological differences and metaphysical and linguistic disputes about the "true" nature of reality. In the end we have an irreconcilable clash of values that colors the frame, context, and logical confines of the debate.

To add to the controversy, there are those who argue that Jung never really had a theory of archetypes at all (see Hogenson, 2004, p. 33), "is a redundant explanation for the origin and transmission of symbols" (Colman, 2015, p. 525), no longer find the term "archetype" necessary, let alone useful (Merchant, 2009), and question if archetypes *really exist*. This is the heart of the matter. Are we merely conjuring up fictions, using language games to define something into existence, or do these processes and presences have an ontological basis? In other words, is the term archetype merely a theoretic fabrication, a social construction, a semiotic—not a reality, hence a signifier rather than a concrete entity in its own right? Even if they are "immaterial entities," as Robert Segal (2014) prefers to call them, we are still left with the task of defining their ontological constraints. These are the philosophical questions I wish to explore in our investigation that follows.

What becomes important to delineate is the *ground* from which an archetype emerges. It can't just pop-up *ex nihilo* without importing some supernatural edifice that is philosophically encumbered unless we rethink the notion of a priori universalism. Emergence cannot happen independently of our embodiment, either materially within our biology or within our concrete social milieus, for psyche is enmattered and resides within place. In other words, archetypes cannot logically or categorically pop into existence from some ephemeral vapor or magical realm. They must be explained as deriving from an organic developmental process that is compatible with reason and science, even if we are engaging the humanities, namely, the human sciences.

The appearance of archaic ontology

When we posit archaic ontology, we evoke the notion of initiation, of *arché* (ἀρχή), hence origins. Psychic and cultural phenomena must have a prehistory, preconditions that stand in relation to their original instantiations. Following the principle of sufficient reason, every mental event must stand in relation to an archaic object that is derived from its original ground. In other words, all psychic experience must stand in relation to its origins. This is the prototype of the unconscious. If an archetype is an original exemplary model or participatory template in which human experience correlates to in some manner, if not emanates from, then we are invoking the question, ground, and scope of original ontology. Here, the meaning of the archetypal must contend with what I call the "genesis problem" (Mills, 2002a) in order to explain how mental activity participates of earlier derivatives and repetitions of original being that may be said to have derived from archaic societies laid down within a collective transpersonal process (even if genetically, developmentally, and culturally transmitted) that conditions how we come to perceive and experience our contemporary world.

Setting aside for the moment the issue of a collective unconscious that informs the psychic development of the human race, which is presumably the womb of archetypal process—Plato's *chora*, here I am mainly interested in pursuing a narrow scope of inquiry into defining and articulating the *essence* of an archetype. In other words, how is it structurally constituted? What are its internal configurations, blueprints, and functional dynamics? Why should we presuppose it in the first place? Does it prove itself? Does it demonstrate its existence? Does it have a source or point of origination? These are not easy questions to answer, because it requires us to speculate about pre-appearances. Whence do archetypes appear? What precedes manifestation? From where do they originate? In order for something to be truly archetypal, would it not have to stand in relation to its pre-manifestation from a primal ontic ground? That which manifests simply does not happen *ex nihilo*, but rather must issue forth from an a priori state of being. That which affirms the recapitulation of the archaic must also implicitly disclose its essence through the reiteration of appearance, hence the replication of original presence.

Extending Eliade's (1949) notion of the repetition of the "mythical instant of the beginning" (p. 35), What would constitute an archetype *ab origine*? Not only would psychic experience stand in relation to its fundamental prototype, namely, *original form*, the manifestation of experience itself would, by necessity, participate of a *prior* organizing principle. Whether this organizing principle derives from a supraordinate systemic process is another matter, a question we may bracket for the moment. Furthermore, if we presume an archetype—if it exists—reflects an original form, would it not also come from conditions that allowed it to arise in the first place, its pre-beginnings, so to speak, that which are *pre-formed*?

This would imply that original form derives from earlier ontic constituencies. But, for the time being we do not know what those conditions would be other than what our speculations have to offer abductively based on what presents itself as evidential. While Jung postulated the collective unconscious, in the end, this may be superfluous, if not simply begging the question. Yet, the metaphysics of origins demands a careful analysis of what *appears* in the collective life of humankind—across societies, geography, and time; and that is arguably more substantive and experientially realized through phenomena we attribute to archetypal process.

Regardless if we can adequately answer to the question of genesis, if we stay focused on the nature of the archetypal, how would the process or mechanism of manifestation work? We must first start with what appears and via abduction attempts to provide a viable or plausible account of how appearance arises from its historicity, viz. original essence. In fact, we must first insist on a first principle, namely, that something comes from something. If we do not, then there is no metaphysical connection to the past. I find this thesis untenable, because the archaic primacy of the past is the ontic precursor that conditions the present. The archaic is a priori ground for which nothing could manifest without it.

What becomes important, I suggest, is to differentiate (at least categorically) the phenomenon of archetypal process from its point of origination; for what appears or manifests to the psyche must be a derivative of an earlier unconscious instantiation that distributes its essence through the modifications in which content, forms, and patterns appear to the subjective mind—whether that be as imagoes, percept, affect, behavioral impetus, the numinous, the mythic, the symbolic, and so forth. Here we must distinguish the (a) *dispersal* of its essence into differentiated and modified modes from the (b) *appearance* of archetypal morphology. Yet we must ask, What transpires *before* the archetype appears? We have postulated that the archetype never appears as such, only its derivatives, so this may be a premature proposition. But what I am getting at is the question of original ground. To tarry with this question further, what are the structures or processes that bring about appearance? In other words, what constitutes the formal parameters of an archetype in the beginning? Here appearance and essence may not be ontologically separated, for essence conditions appearance,[1] although archetypal manifestation may be considered to be a modification of original form.

Let us start from the standpoint of speculative metaphysics. Assume for the moment that an archetype is self-constitutive, that it is a process system or psychic "entity," as Jung calls it,[2] with its own internal pulsions and dynamics in its own right. What if archetypes were autochthonous, what we may say is indigenous to the psyche and derived from its own primordial source? What if archetypes are "parthenogenically born … as self-revelations of the psyche" (Mogenson, 1999, pp. 129–130)? What if archetypes were begotten from themselves, that is, each archetype is a generative *replicator* that exudes its essence into concrete manifestations of appearance—the image, for example? What if archetypes are "autonomous," as Jung says (*CW*, 9, p. 40; *CW*, 11, p. 469),[3] behaving "autocratically" as "involuntary manifestations of unconscious processes" (*CW*, 9, pp. 154, 153, § 260) that spontaneously arise as self-creative acts, and can generate their own productions in our consciousness, engendered from an unconscious ground no less? If this is possible, then the concept of the collective unconscious is not required as the generator of archetypes, for archetypes would be propagative and self-producing. In other words, the collective unconscious would be gratuitous, hence not needed to explain the phenomena of archetypes. This would imply that archetypes ground their own ground, emanating from a primordial *Ungrund*, so to speak, as ground without a ground.

But here, we encounter the problem of agency. We furthermore have to account for causation, unless we are willing to grant the archetype its own spontaneous productions as self-determinative activity, which would further answer to the question of agency, for self-spontaneous generation is an agentic act. But if we cannot justify this metaphysical leap to agency, then the most we can attribute to the archetype is the character of an artifact—as re-production, a repetitive object or datum for consciousness, despite the fact that it carries its own meaning and message, which must be deciphered, unless meaning is relegated to the interpretation and projection of the subject. But when we import the language of hermeneutics, we have already entered into the domain of a dynamic complexity that has a certain degree of teleology, indeed, a particular *intent* no less, for purpose and meaning are conveyed in the very act of production itself. So, when Jung proclaims that archetypes may possess a mythic character or are symbolically infused motifs as *représentations collectives* (*CW*, 5; *CW*, 8: p. 122; pp. 152, 155; *CW*, 9, p. 41), we have already entered the domain of language and communicative action, for all meaning structures convey a conceptual scheme, a message, purposefully I might add, as informational exchange.

When archetypes achieve the complexity of the symbolic, even if dominated by sense perceptions, emotionality, and desire, they convey a meaning that is semiotically charged, for all symbols are linguistically mediated and convey advanced telic properties that are part and parcel of their signification, especially when signification is overdetermined. This means that human language pervades an archetype if it possesses symbolic meaning. If it is not symbolic, it would by definition correspond to less organized and unarticulated emergent properties. And when human language is involved, even when positing archaic humanity, this would imply a collective or cultural process that is agentically informed. Here, once again, enters the question of a collective unconscious, or perhaps merely an archetypal process that is unconsciously organized, self-produced, and dispersed into psychic reality as the coming to presence of earlier forms and potencies. But regardless of the depth or stratification we attribute to unconscious process (individual or collective), it belongs to the universal features of the human psyche, hence a general and unanimous aspect of all people worldwide regardless of gender, race, culture, geography, and time. Because of the presumed universality of the archetype, regardless of the endless modes in which it appears, we may expect to find even more basic configurations that form its structure and meaning networks by closely analyzing its systemic components, that is, the mechanisms involved in the generation of appearances.

On the inner constitution of an archetype

When positing the notion of original ground, what can we discern from closely examining the inner constitution of an archetype? We would expect to find some discernable configuration if the concept of an archetype has any internal consistency; and we would most certainly expect to find empirical evidence for its appearance. But, what about internal consistency?

Before we can answer to this question, we must first define what we mean by interiority.

Unlike Wolfgang Giegerich (1998) who views the soul as pure thought (logical life) grounded in "absolute interiority or internal infinity" (p. 18),[4] here I wish to show how internality emerges from itself and conditions all psychic productions. Interiority means anything that belongs to the inner constitution and experiential life of a complex organization or entity, whether organic or not. It possesses its own internal structures and dynamic relations, is in constant flux and movement, and as such is a temporal-spatial systemic process of becoming. As becoming, psyche founds itself as internal relata through an ensuing series of spacings within its unconscious abyss (Mills, 2002b, 2010). What is at stake here is a speculative metaphysics of postulating the internal workings of a complex system that is self-constitutive, self-organized, and oriented toward communicative exchange, namely, the tendency to disperse its presence and essential contents into other psychic mediums. Here, I am mainly thinking of internal unconscious organizations of quasi-autonomous units of experience as variegated schemata within the individual minds of human subjects within a collective society.

On universality

If we proceed from the premise that archetypes are "universal" (Jung, 1951, p. 585), and that they originate from archaic humanity, what has historically been referred to pejoratively as "primitive man," then we must conclude that they are endemic to human nature, even if they appear in pluralistic (even incompatible or antagonistic) varieties. Here, archetypes are simply rife. We encounter them every day as part of our perfunctory rituals interpassively submersed in unconscious cultural conditioning. But, what can we say about generalities? On the face of things, we must first appeal to universal features. What is an archetype in our most common understanding? Starting with Jung (1957, p. xliv), we import content into any definition, e.g., the archetypal image. But what precedes content? What a priori structures condition the appearance of content?

If an archetype presages and signifies form, then what do we make of a generic form that is formless? Here, we have no discernable content other than the content of amorphous form, a redundant generic category grafted onto a theoretical principle of explaining phenomena. If this is the case, then we are left with analyzing *formless form*. Then what is the ground—the essence—of an archetype if it is merely featureless form? Although we know it as appearance in all its multidimensional and subtle manifestations, we must conclude that formless form constitutes its basic ontological structure. Whether this is an empty formalism is another matter. On the one hand, archetypal form by definition is populated with content, for its own form serves as the foundation of its content, but with stipulations. On the other hand, its generic (universal) structure conforms to *essential factors* that allow for content to manifest. In other words, it must have certain conditions *necessarily*, without which it could not exist. What are such formal parameters? Let us first begin with its universality.

There are at least six classifications we may attribute to the definition of *universal*: (1) totality, entirety; complete; whole; (2) an ontological assertion of absolute inclusion; (3) a general category of participation; (4) a unification principle; (5) infinity or eternal presence; and (6), undifferentiation or an undivided unity. It is mainly within this last class of universality I wish to situate my argument of interiority as the coming into being of internal experience from immediate autochthony as undifferentiated unity to the dispersal of differentiated internality into psychic presence and the particularity of appearance. Therefore, an archetype emerges from its own initial, distinctionless universality. As such, it is its own essence that grounds its own ground.[5] What this means is that an archetype is a freely determinative process system: it not only is its own ground and is grounded, but it gives itself form, substance, and content.[6]

We have argued that an archetype derives from original form, that is, the primordial instantiation of archaic ontology. As the reiteration of archaic form, archetypes condition the individual and cultural productions that populate psyche and society. This would make archetypes a universal phenomenon, and not merely relegated to particularized, personal idiosyncrasies or cultural relativity, for they must be common to all human beings. In fact, it becomes important to underscore the point that in order for there to be any common universality, there must be an essential structure to make anything what it is—without which it would not be. Hence the doctrine of essence is the most rudimentary theoretic that structurally and ontologically fortifies the conditions of being and becoming.[7] What this means is that the universal conditions the particular.

On form and appearance

What is particularly universal is not its content, which varies widely throughout human civilization, but rather the form of an archetype as such, which we have hitherto said is featureless or formless in its generic composition. This gives rise to a special type of universality, namely, a *formless pervasiveness* as a *featureless absolute*. As a universal, it is both pervasive and absolute, for anything short of an all-encompassing ubiquity and totality would annul its universal character. But, how can form be formless when by definition it displays organization as well as a mode or type of configuration? Here, formlessness merely signifies its lack of a specific or defining content; yet this does not mean it lacks defining properties, even if the question of content is suspended for the time being.

Perhaps this featureless form is not so empty after all, insofar as something elementary must exist in order for there to be essence, without which it cannot be nor appear. What we can reasonably conclude at this point, as nebulous as it remains so far in our investigation, following from its a priori constitution, an archetype *must* appear. In fact, an archetype is the appearance of archaic ontology, for nothing can exist unless it is made actual. In Hegel's (1812) language, *"Essence must appear... Existence; it is a being that has come forth from negativity and inwardness ... whatever is, exists.* (pp. 479, 481, italics in original). What the archetype manifests as, however, is content: it is never revealed in its bare formalism. We may only discern this form logically. But the more audacious claim is that archetypal appearance is actually the thing-in-itself—what appears is real or actual as the unveiling and instantiation of essence in its modes of manifestation. Here, the Kantian *noumena* or Fichtean *Anstoss*—the limit, boundary, or rigid check—is superseded by the mere fact that we can posit it. In fact, there is nothing we can know more certain than the essence of the real, for in order to conceive of it or think it at all presupposes that we already know it by virtue of the fact that we posit it.[8]

If we adopt the notion that every manifestation (content) must stand in ontic relation to its original ground (essential form), then an archetype transcends the phenomenal, for it predates appearance as such, hence standing for an *ultimate reality* or *source* from which phenomena manifest, namely, that which conditions all experience. Although appearance and ground are equiprimordial, we can never *experience* the archetype in-itself, as if we could slip into its empty form or encounter the ground from which it emerges, even though we may claim to know it exists. In this respect, it is merely a Platonic Ideal or Hegelian Absolute—simply an idealized abstraction of thought. In other words, we may claim to know it but we do not experience it directly in its original form. So, there has to be a process where appearance stems from ground, which would by logical extension echo back to its archaic organization, as the reverberation of unconscious ontology, which informs the conditions for appearance as such. This transcendental character to the archetype makes the metaphysics of experience interdependent upon an archaic past that conditions the present, although we may argue that it does not necessarily make an archetype deterministic, only determinative.

On essence

Let us now return to the notion of essence. What would constitute a formal organization of archaic form that precedes appearance? In other words, what types of configurations, associations, orders, properties, and functions would an archetype possess, necessarily so, to the degree that it is essential to its nature, without which it would not and could not exist? The question of ontological necessity is so indispensably important that an archetype would never be able to become or reveal itself as the modification or expression of its original instance or act of initial being. In other words, there would be no phenomenology without ontology. You cannot have appearance without some original archaic ground or systemic order (as unconscious process) conditioning the process of becoming. Everything is process, but it must come from prior organizations that are historically constituted as encroachments from the real, the traumatic realization that there are objective facts and events that fracture and intrude on our lived (psychological and material) realities.

We have determined that an archetype possesses the attribute of universality, which is pervasive and absolute, yet it is simultaneously singularly constituted, for each archetype has its own unique character when it discloses itself (i.e., as image, emotion, motif, etc.). This would seem to suggest that each archetype begins as a self-enclosed, self-contained original unit. While at first glance this may sound rather circular, monadic, and solipsistic, because archetypes presumably participate of each other's formal essence, viz., that which makes them what they are, without which they would not be, their appearances are only the appearance of singularity and difference—"partly as diversity, partly as *opposition*" (Hegel, 1812, p. 449, italics in original). Jung (1951) presumably echoes this thesis when he says: "If the archetype, which is universal, i.e., identical with itself always and anywhere, is properly dealt with in one place only, it is influenced as a whole, i.e., simultaneously and everywhere" (p. 585). In order for this to be the case, *all archetypes must participate of a common essence.*

Formal essence must start with a shared commonality to all archetypes that exist before division and modification succeed its breach into distinction, particularity, and multiplicity as the coming into being of lived psychic presence. This would make shared essence an ontological feature of all archetypes regardless of how they appear as singular occurrences, hence derivative forms of original form.

Despite their singularity and dispersal of multiplicity, if archetypes share a common essence, they would have the same formal parameters regardless of how they individually appear to the psyche. Archetypal appearance to the psyche—as imago, numinosity, and so forth—signals its *modification* from original form, that is, appearance is *alteration* from its original makeup as such. This would, at the very least, entail a basic division in its internal constitution: division fractures its original unity. Appearance is the coming to presence of a new form where the archetype is no longer simple and undivided. Manifestation is the particularization of content as *event*, whether this be as impulse, affect, percept, and so forth.

This leads us to analyze the form of form. What is the nature or innermost essence of this form? If an archetype is a (1) self-constituted formal unit that is (2) universal in its unconscious a priorism, only to undergo internal modification and manifest as (3) content, we must therefore explain its movement from (a) internal unity to (b) disruption to (c) manifestation. Here, I suggest an archetype must have a basic structure that is dialectically constituted as self-relation, and moreover as self-in-relation, to identity and difference. At first, an archetype has a simply unity which must undergo division, modification, and dispersal into psychic reality: it is destined to disclose itself, to shine forth, to reveal its hidden presence as content in consciousness. The dialectic of identity and difference is therefore inherent to the structure of an archetype, without which it could not appear as particularization. Because archetypal processes do not appear in the same way, but are derived from primordial or archaic forms, they participate of a common ground or essence that lends order to their appearances. In fact, such internal dynamic structures are the very ontic (relational) conditions for archetypes to manifest.

It may be more helpful to view the internal constitution of an archetype as a *process system* rather than a static object, as a presubjective impersonal formalism that generates the multitude and penumbras of experience. It makes no sense to refer to archetypes as "living subjects" as Jung did (*CW*, 11, p. 469), which anthropomorphizes the concept and is simply bad philosophy. To make an archetype a reified subject is to make it a personal agent rather than simply highlighting the teleonomy and teleology that operates within the process system itself. In other words, by stating that archetypes "are not mere objects of the mind, but are also autonomous factors" (*Ibid*), Jung embarrassingly confounds a mental object (concept) with the *function* of how an internal process may *appear* as an exogenous agency, a living subject no less, like homunculi populating the psyche. We can easily become confused about source, ground, and appearance in our internal experiences to the point that we can imagine they emanate from an external mind-independent provenance. This is merely a fantasy fueled by unconscious desire, defense, and conflict. Archetypes are certainly not inner dwarfs pulling the gear-strings of the mind. The appearance of autonomy or alienation of psychic schemata or internal contents should not be equated with personal entities, let alone deified presences, floating about in the psyche and casting a spell on the individual like a voodoo incantation. In viewing an archetype as a presubjective impersonal formalism that is at once both essence and ground, we are highlighting the ontological a priori foundations in which more subjective experiences of the psyche are conditioned, which furthermore transpire within an objective sociological landscape—the minds of collectives.

Let us return to the equiprimordial oscillation of identity and difference that operates dialectically within the unconscious as tarrying moments of negative relata in search of mediation, synthesis, and unification of opposition as a "transcendent function." The notion of a grand synthesis is a logical fallacy and a fantasy the psyche manufactures in its pursuit of wholeness. But, we can't give up on it because it is a *psychic need* to achieve ideality. We never achieve wholeness. What would that be like? It would mean the end of process, the death of the dialectic of desire. The most we can do is *conceive* of wholeness as a logical culmination of imagination. In Hegel's (1830) apt conclusion, "fantasy is reason" (§ 131).

The dialectic of identity and difference as mutual moments and ontic relations is an indispensable unconscious movement that grounds the ontological makeup of an archetype. From each side, both are immediate and mediate, implicit and explicit, undifferentiated and differentiated in the antediluvian process of seeking a third movement in sublating themselves, hence raising the process to a new complexity, itself a new immediacy. This makes the basic configuration of an archetype more of a *bi-unity* with a *dual-aspect* to its internal relations and functions. In fact, simple divisions of identity and difference, subject and object, self and otherness are not rigid polarities or binaries, but rather they are *dynamic relations* that are always in movement and flux, hence accounting for the multiplicity of contents that populate consciousness emanating from a vast underworld of unconscious pulsions, parallel processes, reciprocal encounters, and negotiations in their acts of materialization. Such dynamic relational exchanges are therefore defined and articulated through their dialectical engagements, not as a bicameral structure, but rather as a mutually communicative exchange of opposing forces that are necessarily interdependent, ontically indivisible, communally implicative, and reciprocally conjoined. I argue this is a fundamental tenet of all psychoanalytic schools.

Archetypes as unconscious schemata

In *Origins: On the Genesis of Psychic Reality*, I offer a formal psychoanalytic metaphysics articulating the birth of psychic agency. Unconscious mind is a *series of spacings* that first instantiate themselves as a multitude of *schemata*, which are the building blocks of psychic reality. A schema is a desirous-apperceptive-ideational unit of self-experience that is teleologically oriented and dialectically constituted. Schemata may be viewed as microagents with semi-autonomous powers of telic expression that operate as self-states as they create spacings within the unconscious mind. Schemata may take various forms, from the archaic to the refined, and materialize as somatic, sensuous, affective, perceptual, and conceptual (symbolic) orders within the psyche, each having their own intrinsic pressures, valences, intensities, intentional and defensive strategies, and unconscious qualia.

The microdynamics of schematic expression can be highly individualistic in their bid for freedom, creativity, complexity, and agentic intent, and are tantamount to the instinctual, desirous, and defensive processes we are accustomed to attribute to unconscious mentation in general. The difference here is that schemata are inherently both free and determined, or perhaps more appropriately, freely determined, that is, they are self-constituted and determinate within the natural parameters in which they find themselves and operate. This means that schematic expression is highly contextual and contingent; yet schemata exist in a multiplicity of process systems that commune, interact, and participate in a society of events that mutually influence the unique constitution of each schematic structure within the sea of the mind. This overdetermination of psychic processes ensures that unconscious agency ultimately underlies the constitution of all mental functioning.

I wish to apply this conceptual scheme to the nature of an archetype. In my language, an archetype would be tantamount to an unconscious schema. There are two general theoretical frameworks we can adopt. One is that we merely assume archetypes are forms and fantasies with desirous-affective-image properties that are generated by the mind derived from unconscious genesis. This view could conceivably be compatible with both Freudian and Jungian conceptions of the unconscious. The second option is that we adopt another speculative framework that attributes the powers of self-generation to the archetype itself. If an archetype is "autonomous" and self-constituted, as Jung contends, are we not justified in attributing a modicum of agency to its inner constitution? While I would not want to attribute selfhood to the constitution of an archetype, as if it were a self, subject, or personality in its own right, strictly speaking, this would not rule out the possibility of agency with the capacity for determinate expression. In fact, there is a certain degree of teleology inherent to an archetype, because it is oriented to express itself, to reveal itself in consciousness, to disclose itself from concealment in its quest to become manifest. Although an archetype is not a proper agent, it nevertheless exudes and executes agency by the mere fact that it appears in the psyche and in all societies. An archetype is therefore a paradigmatic prototype or exemplary model oriented to repeat itself as archaic form in psychic productions.

There is a certain independence in an archetype's capacity toward self-assertion—to impose its presence on psychic reality. In other words, even if archetypes are self-states or quasi-microagents that cluster into their own autonomous organizations in the mind, they have their own internal relations and telic modes of expression. By applying the notion of unconscious schemata as a telic experiential process of self-manifestation, we may potentially explain how archetypes manifest from their primordial ontology. Let us first start with origins, from pre-beginning, the unconscious cosmogonic act of creation.

Because archetypes cannot just appear or blink into existence *ex nihilo*, as we have argued, they must emerge from a primal dynamic ground of self-experience. At the very least we can say is that archetypes must derive from an unconscious organizing principle that is internally impelled to materialize, that is, to become, and is hence subject to being apprehended in consciousness, or otherwise archetypes would never appear. Because of its innate autonomy to manifest, this means that an archetype by necessity would have an agentic character with a particular telos, which accounts for its multiplicity of forms or patterns as well as its specific contents, themes, qualities, valences, intensities, and so forth. We may further speculate that because of its autonomous character, it is self-derived and self-activating, for without which, it would not be released from its unconscious slumber or primal hiddenness. In other words, without such an agentic disposition or proclivity to project or externalize itself into psychic reality, it would not appear. The point here is that in order for an archetype to properly exist, it must make itself actual through determinative action as the *coming into being of internal presence*.

An archetype is construed to be an internal presence, first and foremost as a summonsing of the interior, but we do not know exactly *why* it radiates its essence, if there is a prior supraordinate force, field, or system directing the process, and/or what its essence really signifies, only that its *source* is from within. Those claiming, as Jung did, that archetypes are transpersonal, cosmic external occurrences or organizations superimposed on our interior have a messy epistemological burden to reckon with. Tacking on a collective unconscious agent/creator or transsubjective entity only anthropomorphizes the construct and further problematizes the question of origins by conjuring up a supernatural macroanthropos (Mills, 2013a). It may prove more fruitful to stay focused on how emergence may transpire from internality as this is all we can directly know epistemically as phenomenal-near inner experience. Here, we only need to adopt the theoretic standpoint of internally derived activity to show its logical coherence, for appearance descends and springs from its prior dialectical movements. Before appearance, before archetypal manifestation, we must posit primordial ground as the a priori condition for the unfolding of unconscious phenomenology. Rather than solicit a collective supernatural process where archetypes are said to stem, we may more modestly begin with a naturalized account of psychic phenomena derived from unconscious organizing principles governing internal psychological dynamics. Rather than import the philosophical implications of emanationism or supervenience (see Mills, 2014a), what is more plausible is that internal phenomena condition our metaphysical postulates. While Jung would most certainly agree with this, his incongruities on the nature of the collective unconscious cloud a proper appreciation of the exact nature and essence of what constitutes an archetype. Proceeding from the proposition that archetypes are in essence internal presences, this is much less problematic than asserting their mind independent existence under the rubric of metaphysical realism.

If we succeed in attributing a modicum of agency to the inner constitution of an archetype, then an archetype must have a motive—a telos, as aim—to reveal itself, to express or externalize itself, to make its presence felt and known. In this regard, it is no different than the unconscious desire to fulfill a wish; and it does so by objectifying itself, that is, by making itself an object for consciousness.

Archetypes arise in psyche, for *us*; but *how* do they arise? In other words, what is the mechanism or process that precedes their appearance in consciousness? If archetypes are self-activating, then they must emerge from their own ground. In the beginning, I suggest, an archetype is a self-enclosed unity that must undergo internal division via splitting by its own hands in order to externalize itself from its unconscious void of indeterminateness. This would require an initial act of self-posit or self-assertion where it would rouse or stir itself from indeterminateness to determinate being, that is, from unconscious parallax to conscious presence, from inarticulate implicitness to articulated explicitness in the psyche.

In its initial awakening as self-arousal, an archetype must first take itself as its own content, which is at first its own simple unity, its original form. In taking its original form as its initial content, it performs its own self-mediation as a dialectical enactment of instituting differentiation into its form, which becomes the initial movement from a self-enclosed universality to a differentiated identity as the dispersal of particularity, the instantiation of its essence into psychic reality. This initial act of differentiation and modification becomes the logical model for further patterns and dialectical relations to transpire as archetypes are released and begin to populate mental life.

Birth of an archetype

Archetypes first must manifest as internal presence before they make their transition or trajectory to external presence, namely, as concrete universals that take many forms, such as collective or anthropological motifs, myths, material productions, art and aesthetic expressions, social institutions, cultural organizations, civilizations' ideals, religious beliefs, customs, rituals, and so on. These examples are the *derivatives* of archetypes. Archetypes first manifest as unconscious subjectivity only to become more rich and robust in content, schemata, and *patternings* when breaching into consciousness and objectified in individual personality and the semiotic-socio-symbolic structures that define and govern any culture.

If an archetype is, at its most basic configuration, a patterning of a universal process, then such patterning cannot contain an empty formalism without jeopardizing the integrity of the theory. Rather, I argue, the patterning of an archetype arises from its own internal divisions and splitting maneuvers that naturally introduce mediation between oppositions. Such mediations are two-way internal relations that properly belong to the dialectical form of an archetype that bears a basic structural content as the bi-functionality of identity and difference.

When an archetype arouses itself through rupture from its self-enclosed slumber to the self-certainty of its own pre-reflective being, from implicitness to explicitness, it apprehends itself as unconscious apperception, the coming to presence of its inchoate simple form. In this initial act of apperception, an archetype performs a presubjective determination of instituting differentiation from its previous unmodified shape via reflection into itself, which raises itself to a determinate being-for-self as mediated self-certainty. Here, the apperceptive act of arousal simultaneously is the conferral of its own discrete identity that it sets over itself in relation to all particularities of difference. Opposition becomes the internal dynamic in which dialectical mediation takes place, which is ontically conjoined as an interplay between identity and difference. As an archetype intuits itself as an apperceptive being, it gives itself identity that stands in relation to otherness, an otherness that is necessary in order to concretize the act of self-definition as the awaking of its essence as an internal impetus to manifest. Here, we may say that an archetype originally becomes aware of itself as a pre-reflective burgeoning subjectivity, what we may call an *unconscious self-consciousness*, the simple self-apperceptive immediacy of its being.

Why does an archetype have such an internal impetus to manifest? Because it lacks. Because it desires. Here the desire to wake, to apprehend itself, to manifest, is the expression of its own felt-being in relation to lack. This is the prototype of the human psyche. Desire as being-in-relation-to-lack is the initial essential configuration of an archetype, for it wants to *be*, to experience, to become other than its mere self-enclosed unity. This breach into experience as desire to rectify its lack of being is the first expressive act of self-posit, which elevates the archetype to a living process it feels compelled to externalize as the coming into being of its own actual existence. Here, archetypal process is summarized as the need to experience as being-toward-life. Just as an archetype stirs the psyche through emotional seizure, it first experiences its own internal stirring as self-seizure to awaken and externalize its essence as a living process through self-rupture. We may further suggest that this initial act of self-posit is imbued with existential value and carries an emotional tone as it apprehends itself in its awakened self-immediacy.

The organic sequence of such self-instantiation may further be viewed through the lens of a developmental monistic ontology: moving from the upheaval of its own disquieted desire to self-apperception constitutes the birth of an archetype, for which our own consciousness may, in turn, apprehend as a psychic entity or presence populating mental life. Just as an archetype is seized to self-awaken so too is the human mind jarred to feel its internal presence. Of course, we could be speaking generically about raw affect or emotions in general, but the phenomenal experience is qualitatively different. Archetypes feel like they are connected to something outside of or independent from the self despite the fact that they arise from and are encountered within. In this way, we may further say that an archetype is the epitome of otherness, for its experiential announcement and imposition on consciousness is registered as an unfettered event. The epistemology of this seemingly autonomous process is what adds a further layer of uncanniness and numinosity to the experience—if not alienation from its origins, even if we are mistaken or deluded in interpreting the agency of their internal recurrence. When the psyche comes to notice the myriad patterns in which archetypes manifest, a recurrent theme of repetition cannot escape the discerning self-reflective cogito.

The metaphysics of difference: Toward an archetypal theory of alterity

An archetype is originally an Other to itself, the primordial form of otherness, as alienation from its essence or internal nature, only to discover itself in its own process of becoming as a procreant developmental act. Its initial otherness is ontically entwined in the formal structure of opposition it must mediate and dialectically engage through intermediate dynamic relations of participation in differentiating, reconciling, and synthesizing (reuniting) its various schemata or self-states through informational exchange and reflection into itself. The archetype's breach into self-relation via discerning otherness—hence *non-identity* outside of its original, formal solipsistic unity—is the first dialectical movement toward discovering and defining self-identity that is mediated through conferring difference as non-identicalness. In short, the coming to presence of an archetype within psychic reality is initiated by the breaking up of or split in unity. This initial deed of self-assertion, of pure utter announcement, is the procreative act of mind that draws on the original motif of all cosmogonies: what is archetypal is first, the coming into being of Being. To reiterate my point, it bears repeating archetypes represent and stand in relation to psychic origins.

Although archetypes are everywhere in psyche and culture, we must not lose sight of their fundamental significance: they are replications of original form. We may further say they are self-generating replicators or we would not encounter their ubiquity without the antediluvian drive of spontaneous repetition. Civilization is compelled to reproduce them in our psychosocial arrangements that govern human exchange based on the simple fact that we remember and rewrite history in our preoccupation with the past. This sociological observance highlights the primacy of looking back at, revisiting, acknowledging, and even savoring history as an idealized need for nostalgia, not as immediate presence, but as recapitulation, eternal recurrence. This is why the imaginary has such a stronghold over consciousness, for archetypes repeat themselves through images and associative fantasies that are more or less timeless. This notion (or fantasy) of eternal recurrence is the psychomythology the mind generates and gravitates toward in order to confer meaning and ground its being. In this way, following Eliade, archetypes are the foundation and fulfillment of archaic ontology: every reproduction, every repetition stands *in illo tempore* as attempts at duplication and regeneration.

What is the most basic form of regeneration? May I suggest the search for sameness or familiarity within difference, the restoration of the universal, the reiteration of the eternal? To be more accurate, it is the dialectic of desire and difference we reencounter within the process of the need to return, even though this return is prefaced on the pining for novelty in its attempt at renewal. The basic act of cleavage rests on the institution or insertion of difference in mediatory relations. Therefore, the discernment or interjection of difference introduces a bifurcation within original universality that inaugurates the split as a new bi-unity. Looking for sameness or similarity is to look for universality within difference. This ensures that all acts of judgment identify difference in conferring identity, and that differentiation stands in relation to the universal. Differentiation implies otherness, diversity, and opposition, the supersession of unity, the break from oneness, lost origin. The need to return to familiarity is both a self-grounding act of identity and a regenerative function of recapitulating essence. Just as an archetype discovers itself in its otherness, the Other is its externalization from sameness and lost unity. In its otherness, it wants to return to itself, its lost immediacy, yet at the same time seeks the universal in its differentiation. In other words, difference, variety, and plurality signify the Other, the archetype's initial self-instantiation as becoming other to itself. The breaking up of initial unity is tantamount to the cosmogonic act of dispersing its essence into the world. Difference, particularization, and plurality always stand in relation to original form from which it originated; yet in its modification, it still remains ontically interrelated and interdependent upon its original ground or inception.

What is truly archaic or original has an ontic dialectical relation to otherness or difference that is logically and structurally constituted as unconscious process mediated through alterity. Psychic activity rests on a fulcrum of difference and negation to the degree that without an identifiable and discernable Other, any notion of the archaic would be tantamount to simplicity and solipsism, an untenable proposition in our pluralistic world of particularity and contextual difference.

Does an archetype perform a cognitive act? No—unless you consider it a psychological entity in its own right. Is it registered, felt, and perceived by the psyche? Yes. But, is there really any difference between the two? In other words, Is an archetype independent of mind and culture? Not likely. But, does it appear as if it is an autonomous force in the psyche? Epistemologically, categorically (hence logically), and phenomenologically, Yes. But, can we ever really know its metaphysical status? To make an archetype supersensible, as Jung does by invoking Plato's eternal forms, is misguided, I argue, because this gives them a supernatural significance we are in no way capable of verifying (Mills, 2014b). All we can know is naturalized experience, the coming into being of inner presence.

Perhaps it is sufficient to merely relegate the birth of an archetype as a self-mediated movement to an organic process much like we would attribute to self-regulatory teleonomic mechanisms that unfold and control the processes of life or living organisms. If we adopt this philosophy of organism, it would not be inconceivable to extrapolate this model in its application to inanimate systems, as the discipline of physics has certainly taken the liberty of doing, not to mention succeed in applying a speculative metaphysical paradigm under the rubric of scientific acceptability when conceiving of the cosmos as one big systemic exchange of information. If an archetype can be compared to a material atom or energetic particle, then we may rightly call it an "entity" in its own right, as Jung does (*CW* 8, p. 231), or in Whiteheadian (1929) terms, an "actual occasion." If we conceive of archetypes as occasions, as pure events, we can come to know them through their appearances as patterns of original form.[9]

Patternings become the logical prototype for archetypes to manifest, hence giving rise to alterations in content and contextual appearances. Although divisions of otherness, mutually implicative conflicts, and complexes exist within intrapsychic domains of individuals and societies wed to certain worldviews and values that intersubjectively oppose others, alterity also becomes the social manifestation of splits in identity and difference that maintain certain antitheses in our lived experiences and perceptions of the world. This insures that otherness becomes a fulcrum in the construction of identity based upon differentiation and unfamiliarity, the internalization process, and the nature of recognition and relationality toward shared *and* negated identifications and values. Recognition of otherness is an immediate unconscious prehension that is internally registered, pre-reflectively evaluated and compared to self-identity, and hence dialectically mediated as a self–other relation. Here, the *Alien archetype* is only one such appearance of otherness, much like the Shadow, which subsumes the destructive principle of humankind. But, what is alien to us is none other than our own projective identification with our disavowed interiority that is perceived as foreign. Yet, it is precisely this foreignness we come to recognize as our counterpart we identify with in our reacquaintance with lost universality in ourselves. Following Hegel, we come to know who we are by seeing ourselves in the Other's desire as reacquaintance with lack. We see ourselves in the other, our own lost alienated yearning as being-in-relation-to-lack, a return of original form. This is why we are internally divided and often have to confront many occasions of difference and conflict that seek their dialectical solutions through suspending, negating, binding, or unifying opposition. Here, the transcendent function becomes a regathering of the original split in unity synthesized through our reflective acts of apprehending otherness. This ensures that alterity retains a definitive role in the structure and function of archetypes.

Archetypes always evoke the spectra and specter of the Other, for differentiation and difference permeate the penumbral background that informs experience. Original ontology, the metaphysics of beginnings, the historical consciousness of traditional societies—all experience presupposes referents to the Other, namely, archaic mentality of the collective ethos, the cultural symbolic that conditions the historicity of civilizations and race *in memoriam*. This symbolic other is always there, even when concealed, undisclosed, or non-manifest. It is equivalent to the Lacanian real, the residue of the symbolic that remains foreclosed, occluded, residing outside the chain of signification as a remainder of ineffable desire and lack.

The dialectic of the familiar and the foreign always interpenetrates our encounter with otherness. Whether in acceptance or confrontation, alterity stems from the a priori ground of the archaic and is part and parcel of the human condition. This archaic ground is, in fact, an abyss from which all emerges, the psychic underworld that springs forth into familiar unfamiliarity, an uncanny return to home. The Other is the supersession of original unity as particularized plurality only to participate within the One, the encompassing universality that pervades psyche and culture. As an archetype disperses its essence into multiplicity, it becomes other to itself, only to recover its original lost unity in such otherness as a return to itself. In the *arché* is *origo*, an opening, *another*, to arise.

Notes

1 For Hegel (1807, 1817, vol. 1), "appearance is essence" (*PS* § 147); "essence must appear" (*EL* § 131), for nothing can exist unless it is actual, hence it must manifest. Elsewhere, I have shown how Hegel's philosophy of Spirit anticipates psychoanalysis (Mills, 2002b) and that the human psyche is derived from an unconscious abyss, whereby unconsciousness appears as consciousness, its modified and evolved form.

2 In discussing the *unus mundus*, Jung alludes to an archetype as a "transcendental entity" (*CW*, 14, p. 536), what he earlier conceived of as "psychic entities" (*CW*, 8: p. 231).

3 Throughout his *Collected Works*, Jung refers to archetypes acting as autonomous agents within the mind (see Mills, 2013a for a review). In fact, he states that "they are experienced as spontaneous agencies" where their very "nature" is derived from "spirit" (*CW*, 8: p. 216).

4 Although I have read very little of Giegerich's works, what appears at face value is his annexation of Hegel's Logic into his discourse on soul. In *The Soul's Logical Life* (2001), he gives us a clue. In discussing the soul's "complex dialectical logic," he refers to Hegel's "*Science of Logic*, which might serve as a model for the kind of abstract thought required to do justice to the complexities of the plight of the modern soul. Psychology needs the 'labor of the Concept'" (p. 26). Compare to Hegel (1812): "The beginning is *logical* in that it is to be made the element of thought that is free and for itself, in *pure knowing*. It is *mediated* because pure knowing is the ultimate, absolute truth of *consciousness*" (p. 68, italics in original), hence the "labor" of *Begriff*. As Hegel would say, logic is the "absolute ground" (p. 67). Here, Giegerich appears to take Hegel's *Logic* as the starting point of any discussion—from metaphysics to psychology, and then applies the logic of the dialectic to the notion of soul or what we would call the modern day subject or the living personality of each individual's psychological makeup. He

appears to take the extreme stance of absolute interiority as inner infinity (as logical workings) that he privileges over all other aspects of mind—hence thought is preferred over image, affect, imagination, instinct, or action. This amounts to an extreme form of idealism that does not create a mediatory split between inner and outer, only that there is *no outside*. Where does the dialectic go from here? I assume a return to absolute interiorizing. This seems very solipsistic, if not untenable, and is not particularly faithful to Hegel's overall system, because this stance of radical interiority only highlights spirit in particular *moments*. One must question his notion of the absolute autonomy of the psyche, which he equates with absolute negative interiority, a rather omnipotent proposition at that. Here, he seemingly takes Hegel's Logic as the coming into being of pure self-consciousness through dialectical relata and then applies it narrowly to the internal configurations of the psyche. In Hegel's (1817, vol. 3) system, psychology is the sublation (*Aufhebung*) of the soul (*Seele*), which he articulates in his section on Theoretical Spirit in the *Encyclopaedia of the Philosophical Sciences*. The feeling soul is a general, affective unconscious condition of the psyche that dialectically unfolds and raises itself to the standpoint of cognition and psychological dynamism. But Logic conditions all of this, like the biblical *Genesis*. *Geist* is pure thought (kind of like God) that disperses its essence into the materiality of nature (creation) (see 1817, vol. 2); and then the soul (outlined in the Anthropology section of the *Encyclopaedia*) is the germination of the human spirit that developmentally makes its way dialectically from its material embodiment (as an incipient mind—here more like an infant) to the ego of consciousness as subjectivity (consciousness); and then proceeds in the Phenomenology (1807, 1830) from subjective mind (the inner workings of each conscious being) to objective mind (society and worldhood), only to come full circle to culminate in Absolute unity in full self-consciousness as world spirit realized through the Idea or Concept of the process of its own becoming as pure knowing—hence pure thought thinking about itself and all its operations. And yet, this is the return to itself as the culmination and fulfillment of its Logical nature as pure thought thinking itself into being and fulfilling its own development as a spiritual–mental force grounded in a rational process. Perhaps Absolute Spirit is something similar to the concept of the *anima mundi* within the *unus mundus*, but more impersonal.

5 In Hegel's (1812) *Wissenschaft der Logik*, he is very clear: "*Essence determines itself as ground*" (p. 444, italics in original).

6 Cf. Hegel (1812): "Ground is first, *absolute ground*, in which essence is, in the first instance, a substrate for the ground relation; but it further determines itself as *form* and *matter* and gives itself a *content*" (p. 445, italics in original).

7 In Hegel's (1812) *Wesenslogik*, he states, "The truth of *being is essence*" (p. 389, italics in original).

8 Cf. Hegel (1812): "Appearance is that which the thing is in itself, or its truth" (p. 479).

9 We may perhaps, not inappropriately, follow a similar formula as the discipline of physics that claims to have discovered the Higgs field through inference and indirect evidence.

References

Colman, W. (2015). A revolution of the mind: Some implications of George Hogenson's 'The Baldwin Effect: A neglected influence on C.G. Jung's evolutionary thinking' (2001). *Journal of Analytical Psychology*, 60(4): 520–539.

Colman, W. (2016). *Act and Image: The Emergence of Symbolic Imagination.* New Orleans, LA: Spring Publications.

Eliade, M. (1949). *The Myth of the Eternal Return.* Princeton, NJ: Princeton University Press.

Freeman, J. (1959). *Face to Face* (Interview with C.G. Jung). Produced by the BBC.

Giegerich, W. (1998). Is the soul "Deep?": Entering and following the logical movement of Heraclitus' "Fragment 45." *Spring*, 64: 1–32.

Giegerich, W. (2001). *The Soul's Logical Life*, 3rd Revised Ed. Frankfurt am Main: Peter Lang.

Goodwyn, E. (2010). Approaching archetypes: Reconsidering innateness. *Journal of Analytical Psychology*, 55: 502–521.

Goodwyn, E. (2013). Recurrent motifs as resonant attractor states in the narrative field: A testable model of the archetype. *Journal of Analytical Psychology*, 58: 387–408.

Hegel, G.W.F. (1807 [1977]). *Phenomenology of Spirit*, (trans. A.V. Miller). Oxford: Oxford University Press.

Hegel, G.W.F. (1812/1831 [1969]). *Science of Logic.* (Trans. A.V. Miller). London: George Allen and Unwin Ltd.

Hegel, G.W.F. (1817/1827/1830 [1991]). *The Encyclopaedia Logic*, Vol.1 of the *Encyclopaedia of the Philosophical Sciences*, (trans. T.F. Geraets, W.A. Suchting, and H.S. Harris). Indianapolis: Hackett Publishing Company, Inc..

Hegel, G.W.F. (1817/1827/1830 [1970]). *Encyclopaedia of the Philosophical Sciences.* Vol. 2: *Philosophy of Nature.* (Trans. A.V. Miller). Oxford: Clarendon Press.

Hegel, G.W.F. (1817/1827/1830 [1971]). *Encyclopaedia of the Philosophical Sciences.* Vol. 3: *Philosophy of Mind.* (Trans. William Wallace and A.V. Miller). Oxford: Clarendon Press.

Hegel, G.W.F. (1830 [1978]). *Philosophy of Spirit.* In M.J. Petry (Ed.), *Hegel's Philosophy of Subjective Spirit.* Vol. 3: *Phenomenology and Psychology.* (Trans. and Ed. M.J. Petry). Dordrecht, Holland: D. Reidel Publishing Company.

Hillman, J. (2013). *Archetypal Psychology*, 4th Ed. Putnam, Connecticut: Spring Publications.

Hogenson, G.B. (2001). The Baldwin effect: A neglected influence on C.G. Jung's evolutionary thinking. *Journal of Analytical Psychology*, 46(4): 591–611.

Hogenson, G.B. (2004). Archetypes: Emergence and the Psyche's deep structure. In J. Cambray and L. Carter (Eds.), *Analytical Psychology: Contemporary Perspectives in Jungian Analysis* (pp. 32–55). New York: Brunner-Routledge.

Hogenson, G.B. (2009). Archetypes as action patterns. *Journal of Analytical Psychology*, 54(3): 325–337.

Jones, R.A. (2000). On the empirical proof of archetypes: Commentary on Maloney. *Journal of Analytical Psychology*, 45: 599–605.

Jung. C.G. (1953–1977). *Collected Works of C.G. Jung*; Bollingen Series, 20 vols. Eds. H. Read, M. Fordham, G. Adler; Trans. R.F.C. Hull. London: Routledge & Kegan Paul; Princeton: Princeton University Press. (hereafter referred to *CW* by vol. no.)

Jung. C.G. (1911–1912). *Symbols of Transformation, CW*, 5.

Jung. C.G. (1916). *The Relations Between the Ego and the Unconscious. CW*, 7: pp. 121–241.

Jung. C.G. (1919). Instinct and the Unconscious. *CW*, 8, pp. 129–138.
Jung. C.G. (1934/1954). Archetypes of the collective unconscious. *CW*, 9, pt.1:pp.3–41.
Jung. C.G. (1936/1942). Psychological factors determining human behaviour, *CW*, 8, pp. 114–125.
Jung. C.G. (1937). *Psychology and Religion. CW*, 11: pp. 3–200.
Jung. C.G. (1940). The psychology of the child archetype. *CW*, 9: pp. 151–181.
Jung. C.G. (1947). On the nature of the psyche. *CW*, 8: pp. 159–234.
Jung. C.G. (1951/1973–1975). *Letters of C.G. Jung. Vol. II: 1951–1961*. London: Routledge and Kegan Paul.
Jung. C.G. (1952). Synchronicity: An acausal connecting principle. *CW*, 8: pp. 417–531.
Jung. C.G. (1952b). Answer to job. *CW*, 11: pp. 355–470.
Jung. C.G. (1955). *Mysterium Coniunctionis. CW*, 14.
Jung. C.G. (1957). Psychological commentary. In W.Y. Evans-Wentz (Ed.) *The Tibetan Book of the Dead, 3rd Ed* (Trans. R.F.C. Hull). Oxford: Oxford University Press, pp. xxxv–lii.
Jung. C.G. (1961). *Memories, Dreams, Reflections.* New York: Vintage.
Jung. C.G. (Ed.) (1964). Approaching the unconscious. *Man and His Symbols.* New York: Doubleday, pp. 18–103.
Knox, J.M. (2003). *Archetype, Attachment, Analysis.* London: Brunner-Routledge.
Merchant, J. (2009). A reappraisal of classical archetype theory and its implications for theory and practice. *Journal of Analytical Psychology*, 54(3): 339–358.
Maloney, A. (1999). Preference ratings of images representing archetypal themes: An empirical study of the concept of archetypes. *Journal of Analytical Psychology*, 44: 101–116.
Mills, J. (2002a). Deciphering the "Genesis Problem": On the dialectical origins of psychic reality. *The Psychoanalytic Review*, 89(6), 763–809.
Mills, J. (2002b). *The Unconscious Abyss: Hegel's Anticipation of Psychoanalysis.* Albany: State University of New York Press.
Mills, J. (2010). *Origins: On the Genesis of Psychic Reality.* Montreal: McGill-Queens University Press.
Mills, J. (2013a). Jung's Metaphysics. *International Journal of Jungian Studies*, 5(1), 19–43.
Mills, J. (2013b). Freedom and determinism. *The Humanistic Psychologist*, 41(2), 101–118.
Mills, J. (2014a). *Underworlds: Philosophies of the Unconscious from Psychoanalysis to Metaphysics.* London: Routledge.
Mills, J. (2014b). Jung as philosopher: Archetypes, the Psychoid factor, and the question of the supernatural. *International Journal of Jungian Studies*, 6(3), 227–242.
Mills, J. (2017). *Inventing God: Psychology of Belief and the Rise of Secular Spirituality.* London: Routledge.
Mogenson, G. (1999). Psyche's archetypes: A response to Pietikainen, Stevens, Hogenson and Solomon. *Journal of Analytical Psychology*, 44(1): 125–134.
Pietikainen, P. (1998). Archetypes as symbolic forms. *Journal of Analytical Psychology*, 43: 325–343.
Saunders, P. and Skar, P. (2001). Archetypes, complexes and self-organization. *Journal of Analytical Psychology*, 46, 305–323.

Segal, R.A. (2014). On Mills' 'Jung's Metaphysics.' *International Journal of Jungian Studies*, 6(3), 217–226.

Stevens, A. (2002). *Archetype Revisited: An Updated Natural History of the Self.* London: Routledge.

Roesler, C. (2012). Are archetypes transmitted more by culture than biology? Questions arising from conceptualizations of the Archetype. *Journal of Analytical Psychology*, 57, 223–246.

Whitehead, A.N. (1929). *Process and Reality.* Corrected Edition. Ed. D.R. Griffin and D.W. Sherburne. New York: Free Press, 1978.

Chapter 2

Archetypal origins
Biology vs culture is a false dichotomy

Erik Goodwyn

What makes an archetype?

Jung defined the archetype in many ways, depending on the particular context in which he was discussing them. When he focused on the relationship of the individual psyche to the mythic motif, however, Jung was consistent in his contention that the archetypal *image* was merely a token for the deeper archetype-as-such which he asserted we inherited, in the form of an inborn structural predisposition. An example of this approach to the archetype can be found in his essay "The structure and dynamics of the psyche":

> Archetypes, so far as we can observe and experience them at all, manifest themselves only through their ability to organize images and ideas, and this is always an unconscious process which cannot be detected until afterwards.
>
> (Jung 1919, para. 440)

The archetype-as-such is the tendency to *arrange* memories and imaginary contents in a particular way and this tendency, according to Jung, is inherited. Note the distinction, however, is that the *tendency to arrange content* is what is inherited, *not* the contents themselves.

Subsequent scholarship has struggled with this concept of inherited archetypal structures, particularly in light of findings in genetics and developmental psychology. Whereas Jung and others of his day may have believed that certain psychological contents could present themselves "without any environmental input", it is clear today that environmental input is an integral part of the development of the psyche from very early stages. Writers such as Jean Knox (2003), Saunders and Skar (2001), and John Merchant (2009) have noted that human development involves a tremendous amount of environmental input, which appears to lead to the conclusion that Jung was wrong about the archetype-as-such possibly being inherited. A recent article summarizing this debate (Roesler, 2012), presents the question with great clarity: are archetypes transmitted more by culture than biology?

DOI: 10.4324/9781003349921-2

I believe Roesler's paper is very helpful in the way it summarizes the various positions—I have written essays that question the assertion that we need to redefine or eliminate the idea of biologically inherited archetypes-as-such, and so find myself classified as on the "biological" side of this debate. One aspect of my position on this issue, however, has never changed, but strangely it has thus far not garnered as much attention: I continue to believe that the above question, "are archetypes transmitted more by culture than biology?" is *wrongly posed*. In this essay, I will focus the discussion fully on this issue.

Biology, innateness, and genes

What the above question seems to be trying to discern is just how "innate" archetypes-as-such are. Jung obviously thought they were. But some theorists since Jung have been concerned that genetics and epigenetic modification (as in, say, Knox, 2003) rule out this possibility. I have written before about how modern genetics and the facts of epigenetic modification of the genome do *not* require us dismiss the idea of inherited archetypes-as-such. But, even from the very beginning I was puzzled as to why anyone would think that it was required in the first place. Epigenetic modification is ubiquitous in all organisms in all development: it's not as helpful in answering this question as we might like. Genetics can tell us about the effects of the absence or presence of a particular protein, or it can tell us about biomarkers for various mental illnesses, but for more specific questions about psychic contents, genetic influence is more complex to tease out (even ignoring the difficulties of the mind–body problem).

That doesn't mean we can't parse out what is innate and what is not regarding the *psyche*. We have to look at the development of macrostructures and macrobehaviors at the organism level, rather than try to get bogged down in proximate mechanisms giving rise to them. We have to look at the development of convergent skills, functions, reported experiences, particular qualities, and characteristics. Those characteristics which develop reliably and universally, and require no learning to speak of in normally developing humans—like, say, the ability of the heart to pump blood is for the body—are reasonably described as "innate" psychological contents and might be fairly called "transmitted biologically", even if there is massive epigenetic modification, plasticity, and/or emergence along the way (as there no doubt is). Those characteristics that do *not* develop reliably, however, and/or require a significant amount of instruction or mimicry—like, say, the ability to drive a car—should obviously not be called "innate".

Note, however, that some behaviors and corresponding mental contents have *both* innate and learned components to them. The ability to speak and think in *a* language, for example, arises reliably and universally in all normally developing humans. This ability does not, however, arise in frogs. At the most fundamental level, human infants will babble and orient themselves to other humans (usually caretakers), and spontaneously set in motion a cascade of developmental events that ultimately will lead them to understanding and speaking a language over the course of a few years (Orr and Geva, 2015). In other words, keep talking to an infant and eventually she will talk back to you. Frogs, by contrast, will simply croak at you no matter how much you talk to them. It does not require any learning for the infant to begin or continue to support this process, so the *ability* to learn a language in the first place is innate. Finally, while the input of caretakers in the process is very important, it is well known that infants and toddlers continually refine themselves with constant babbling and play-exploration, so self-teaching is a part of the process also (Osório et al., 2012). In much the same way, infants' body motions follow a gradual pattern, beginning with innate, nonspecific (but constant) movement to rolling, to "scooting", to crawling, to pulling up onto things, and then finally to walking. This behavior requires a great deal of learning—but it is *self-directed* learning. Infants and toddlers teach themselves how to do it with constant movement and refinement of coordination, but it does not need to involve mimicry or instruction. We know this because congenitally blind persons manage to acquire spatial navigation strategies just as sighted persons do—they just teach themselves differently how to do it (Schinazi et al., 2016). We therefore cannot call this behavior "transmitted culturally" because they would obviously teach themselves to do it no matter what the culture (more on early blind individuals below). There is therefore nothing specifically *cultural* about this sort of learning.

Thus, if we look at the question "are archetypes transmitted more by culture than biology?", it seems evident that these two options do not exhaust all the possibilities. For the rest of this essay, I will present examples of many psychological contents that fit into neither of these categories. Moreover, I will argue that this fact still gives us *no* reason to cast out Jung's idea of an "inborn" archetype-as-such.

The archetype-as-such: Biology or culture?

So, the question arises: is this tendency a consequence of our biology? Or is it *actually* a result of culture—a case of mimicking/internalizing stories we have encountered? My answer: this is a false dichotomy. There are psychological contents whose origins do not neatly fit into either category, and this becomes evident once you take a closer look at them. But first we must define what exactly we mean by "biologically" or "culturally" transmitted. For purposes of this analysis, I will propose two working definitions:

1   Biologically transmitted: psychological contents which emerge without any significant learning. These contents often appear to be related to our evolutionary history.

2   Culturally transmitted: psychological contents which one acquires from one's surrounding culture—i.e., contents which one learns from observing and/or mimicking others in the environment such as caretakers.

Before I get into contents which do not fit into either of these categories, let's look at some that do. Aside from the above reference to capacity for language, I find that the best and most rigorous evidence base that reveals our innate psychological structures comes from the fundamental neural emotional systems observed and meticulously documented by affective neuroscientists Jaak Panksepp and others (Panksepp, 1998, 2005). These emotional systems are strongly homologous across all mammals and develop with high levels of reliability, likely representing the physiological aspects of the innate infrastructure of the psyche. The core systems affective neuroscientists identify (capitalized per convention) are FEAR, RAGE, LUST, PLAY, CARE, SEEKING, and GRIEF/PANIC. These sophisticated and coordinated systems develop in a strongly convergent and conserved manner in the brain stem subcortical midline regions of humans and other mammals. Most importantly these systems correlate with convergent *psychological experiences* of the emotions in question, as confirmed by direct stimulation studies in humans and other animals (Alcaro et al., 2017: 4; Panksepp, 1998, 2005, *passim*). These centers orchestrate broad behavioral and perceptual modes of sensorimotor integration, though they do not likely have much in the way of specific content. Rather, they strongly emotionally color experience and provide it with a collection of sensorimotor biases and constraints moreso than direct internal imagery.

Interestingly enough, affective neuroscientists have begun to take serious notice of Jung (Alcaro et al., 2017) and subsequent Jungian literature, including that of Anthony Stevens (2003) and myself. They find that Jung's foundational principles relating brain to psyche and archetype "Were not only quite farsighted, but they actually open ways to connect his theory of the psyche with the most advanced scientific theories and discoveries of our day." (Alcaro et al., 2017: 2). They remark that recent affective neuroscientific findings thoroughly corroborate many of Jung's ideas, identifying core affective systems as likely biological dimensions of the archetypes-as-such (Alcaro 2017: 7). Notably, the subcortical midline structures that comprise the core affective systems underlie all conscious experience and share functionality with the affective, coordinating and deeply structuring activity of the Self archetype, just as Jung proposed *and* correlating with the activity of the brain region that he postulated (Alcaro et al., 2017: 10). Humans without these structures do not exist, as their absence is incompatible with life, and lesions in these areas correlate with catastrophic loss of function. The activities of these structures appear to correlate with innate formal and structural elements of the psyche, consciousness, affect, and imagination that nonetheless require personal experience to detail into full-blown images, thus providing innate basic structure with nevertheless wide variation in surface texture. These neural centers are nearly functionally mature at birth, universal in humans and mammals, and thus innate—meaning they correlate with psychological dispositions that require no learning to emerge.

What about culturally transmitted contents? These are much easier to identify—probably because whereas no one remembers the emergence of the innate contents because they arrived well before autobiographical memory can reach, everyone recalls learning something during the course of their lifetime. Various specific skills ranging from baking cookies to memorizing poetry to playing a musical instrument to building a house to solving multivariable calculus problems are all obtained by cultural learning that would be very difficult to acquire without the cultural input. It is presumably this latter category that some theorists argue archetypes-as-such (i.e. the structure of independently invented stories and images) must be acquired. Growing up, we hear various stories and see various symbols, and that is how they are transmitted, rather than having much to do with our internally derived development.

This assumption probably seems reasonable because for so long, imitative learning has often been the default explanation in developmental psychology. For example, a while ago Gallagher (2001) argued that the psychological skill known as theory of mind (understanding the perspective of other minds) is acquired through "imitation, intentionality detection, eye-tracking, the perception of intentional or goal-related movements, and the perception of meaning and emotion in movement and posture" (2001, p. 90). Others (Karmiloff-Smith, 1992, p. 117–138) invoke mutual eye gaze, joint attention, and gaze alternation. Sounds plausible, only *this can't be the way it happens.* How do we know it can't? Because of extensive research on congenitally blind persons, who develop theory of mind capability equal to sighted individuals and along the same timeline (Bedny et al., 2009), which means they acquire it without doing any of the above observation or mimicry. This consideration leads us to the area *in between* the two proposed categories: that is, contents which likely require *some* learning to arise, but nevertheless it is a kind of learning that is not imitative or "cultural" learning. Rather, it is internally directed learning, and it is often implicit.

Contents in neither category

To find examples that fit neither category, I refer to congenital blindness studies frequently in these discussions because this data reveals just how much development is *initiated, internally maintained and internally progressed by the growing individual* rather than dependent upon imitative or culture-specific learning. For example, beyond theory of mind, those born blind have been demonstrated to show normal proficiency in a whole array of perceptual and cognitive skills including facial recognition, number-form recognition, animacy identification, object representation, complex spatial cognition, mirror-neuron system development, intuitive physics, drawing maps and other pictures, mental rotation and much more. These skills develop without subjects having the benefit of seeing anyone else do them, nor is it easy to imagine how many of these skills (such as mental rotation) could be "taught" (see Abboud et al., 2015; Bertolo et al., 2003; Kupers and Ptito, 2011; Mahon et al., 2009; Ricciardi et al., 2009; Renier et al., 2014; Sigalov et al., 2016; Tinti et al., 2006 for reviews). In a 2014 review, neuroscientists Lingnau et al. report that:

> these studies provide converging evidence for the potential of many sensory regions to retain some of their functional characteristics even as the modality of the inputs driving them changes dramatically…the functional specialization of the [sensory subregions of the brain] is thus *experience independent*…neural plasticity acts within a relatively rigid framework of predetermined functional specialization." (546, italics original).

It is tempting to classify these contents as fully innate, however, they do not exactly fit this category because the early blind individuals are, of course, learning—only it is *innately initiated* learning, however, that is essentially *self-generated* and independent of culture, which is why it doesn't fit either category.

Another illustrative phenomenon is the acquisition of emotionally communicative face and body expressions. Several studies have shown that born-blind individuals spontaneously produce culture-independent facial expressions and body language that signify emotional states, including instantly recognizable face/body language associated with happiness, sadness, distress, surprise, disgust, shame, pride, anger, contempt, and levity. If visual experience affects these expressions at all, it is *only* in modulating their intensity; the expressions themselves are innate (Kunz et al., 2012; Matsumoto and Willingham, 2009; Tracy and Matsumoto, 2008). This echoes the observations of affective neuroscientists who state that "experience is more influential in changing the *quantitative* expression of neural systems rather than their *essential nature.*" (Panksepp, 1998: 17). For our purposes, these studies demonstrate strong evidence that visual, imitative (and hence cultural) experience is not necessary to produce these physical representations of inner emotional states—they happen automatically during the course of development and arguably require no imitative learning except in their modulation. Note also that these are *symbolic* expressions—emotions are being represented visually by a facial/body configuration, and they do not depend on visual experience; hence they are innate symbolic associations modulated slightly by imitative/cultural learning. Symbolic thought itself, and play, are other skills that infants and toddlers appear to naturally teach themselves how to do; input from caretakers modulate but do not create this process (Osório et al., 2012).

Thus it seems that there is a third category of content source that involves *self-generated learning* that is only modestly affected by instructional/imitative input, if at all. This fact *must* play into our question about the source of archetypes-as-such. Let's look at some more examples of self-taught contents:

1   The belief that the sun is round. Unlike the purely "biological" examples given above, there is no reason to think that this belief should automatically develop—it requires some learning. The sun, for all we know as children, could, in fact, be banana shaped. Yet, this belief is universal because anyone can simply look at the sun and make the connection themselves. Thus, there is learning involved here, however, there is nothing particularly *cultural* about this learning. Anyone could piece this one together without any help. No one needs to teach you this—you *teach yourself* this fact, and it is this self-teaching (akin to self-organization but in psychological terms) that puts this psychological content in our third category *between* the biological vs cultural.

2   The capacity for metaphor. As mentioned above, the capacity for symbolic thought progresses in a self-generated fashion that is only modestly modulated by caretaker input (McCune, 2010; Orr and Geva, 2015; Osório et al., 2012). As metaphorical thought progresses in early blind individuals just as well as sighted individuals, it may very well be strictly biological—meaning in the sense that it requires no specific learning to obtain (see Goodwyn, 2012: 46–48). But, even if it *is* learned (as Lakoff and Johnson think it is, 1998; see also Lakoff and Turner, 1989; Kövecses, 1986; Pinker, 2007 for varying viewpoints on this subject), there are no aspects of any culture that appear to *need* to teach this extremely important capacity to anyone. Either it develops automatically, or we all teach ourselves to do this during very early development. This capacity develops unconsciously in a self-taught manner and structures much of our subsequent day to day thought. It is true that thinking metaphorically can be elaborated upon to a great extent, much like any language can be learned upon the innate capacity to learn a language. But, we do not need to mimic others using metaphors or obtain specific instruction in it in order to do it ourselves. Symbolic play develops spontaneously around the 18 month age range (McCune, 2010; Osório et al., 2012), however, more recent work is revealing the fact—important for our purposes—that infants play "an active role in their own development" (Orr and Geva, 2015: 159), again emphasizing the self-generated nature of this sort of learning, showing that cultural learning may be sufficient ("mommy said the sun was round"), but it is not *necessary* because of the extremely active role the growing individual plays in her

own learning and development. Interestingly enough, just as I was writing the first draft of this essay, my 18-month old granddaughter began giving my wife and me a semicircular magnet to "drink" from, clearly wanting us to pretend the magnet was a cup of milk, thus using it symbolically. She spontaneously created this game herself and found great joy in it. She had never seen anyone else play with the magnet in this way and so provided me a vivid example of what I was talking about.

3   The idea that anger is "hot". This psychological connection is not one that necessarily must develop automatically without any learning. Nevertheless, because anger itself is universal and biologically innate, and it is associated with increases in body temperature and blood pressure due to its effects on the sympathetic nervous system, it is an association everyone experiences and so the psychological link is one everyone teaches themselves (likely unconsciously) during the course of early development. Nevertheless, like the sun belief, no culture is necessary to teach this to you. You would learn this no matter what culture you grew up in. So, it is an idea that does not require cultural transmission to persist. It will arise anew in each person during normal development. The fact that so many cultures have symbols that equate fire with rage (or with other temperature raising emotions such as lust and seeking) is *not* evidence that this idea is transmitted culturally, rather it is evidence that this idea is extremely easy to teach oneself universally. Since it requires learning, it's not innate in a strict sense (although one could argue it is innate in a broader sense), but it's not classifiable as culturally taught either, in the sense that one *wouldn't* arrive at this idea had one *not* been taught by one's culture to connect these ideas.

4   The impression that high is "better than" low, which leads to all sorts of symbolic associations of verticality with "greater" things. Consider, for example, the countless symbols of the *axis mundi* seen around the world that connects the material world with the divine (and hence superior) world (Eliade, 1958, *passim*). It is conceivable that one could live in a world where low positions lead to better overall success in life than high ones. And yet, as children we all likely learn that "higher up" is better for a number of reasons. First, standing is certainly better than falling in terms of mobility and remaining free from injury. We all learn this during the first few years of life and it becomes implicit memory, and because of this we don't remember learning it. Second, we all also observe that the people in power when we are young are *always* taller than we are, making "up" (and also "big") an easy-to-think symbol for "powerful". Third, higher positions allow for greater vantage points, provide a physical advantage in conflicts, and they give an increased ability to know one's surroundings, whereas being stuck in a hole, frankly, sucks. All of these universal facts reinforce this symbolic association. It doesn't take a unique creative genius to figure this out and pass it on

culturally. Thus, even though this idea requires learning, like the others it does not necessitate any particular "cultural" learning to acquire, especially given the universal tendency toward metaphoric thought. It is abundantly obvious to any normally developing psyche from a very early age.

5   Personification of objects and environments. Like metaphorical thought, personification occurs at an early age, and it likely emerges due to our extremely social nature as cooperative primates, our natural predilection for human faces and verbal communication, as well as our natural desire to try to discern intent in others. All of these innate capacities we learn to use in order to understand the physical world, applying intent and mentality onto objects and locations in the process. Thus it is learned, but it *not* learned imitatively (as the early blindness studies again show us), rather it is something we teach ourselves to do. Again, my granddaughter provided me with another example, as she recently began to ask for a blanket so she could let her teddy bear "go nap". She informed me that the teddy bear was "sleepy", so clearly the bear needed a blanket. No one taught her this game and she hadn't observed anyone doing this with objects. She personified the teddy bear and came up with this herself. She also swatted at the table when she tripped over it, telling it "no!". Plenty of examples like this could be multiplied: we don't have to observe others giving teddy bears a nap for this principle of human thought to naturally occur to a toddler—it is not a part of any specific cultural learning. We teach ourselves to do this and it therefore fits neither category.

6   Light is a metaphor for knowledge, darkness is a metaphor for the unknown. Given our already established self-taught (or innate) tendency to think in metaphors, there is no need to postulate any automatic, learning-independent tendency to connect these two concepts (although one wonders what those born blind do with these metaphors—it's not been studied to my knowledge). Rather, simply by virtue of being diurnal mammals with well-developed visual capabilities, adapted to surviving in environments of moderate to high levels of light, it makes sense that every one of us will make this metaphorical connection without anyone needing to teach us this principle specifically. As metaphors go, the connection is easy, obvious, and universal. To claim it is culturally transmitted, however, would be to claim that we would *not* naturally come to this symbolic connection on our own if someone didn't mention it—this seems very implausible.

7   A circle or sphere is an image of wholeness. This is clearly not a learning-independent idea. Nevertheless, there are certain anatomical facts and basic characteristics of the circular/spherical shape that lend itself to make very easy symbolic associations between the image and the concept. First, circles are basic shapes that children can conceptualize

(again, even those born blind) before age 1 (Karmiloff-Smith, 1992: 67–70; Kupers and Ptito, 2011; Mahon et al., 2009; Tinti et al., 2006), so if this is not an innate concept, it is one that is self-taught early on, and before anyone has memory of doing so. Second, there are features that circles have that lend themselves to metaphorical associations with more abstract ideas of wholeness or integration. The reason is that circles, unlike other shapes, are symmetrical in every direction. This peculiar property naturally would lend itself to be representative of more abstract ideas like "balance" (another self-taught metaphor that, like vertical metaphors, is based on our body kinesthetic sense). This symmetry also serves as a suitable symbolic representation of the integration of many into one—no part "lopsided", no part "out of balance". All parts equally working together within the shape. Note also that the visual field itself is a circle which integrates a large amount of sensory data into a single, tightly-bound sensory event (though again, this may only reinforce the symbol rather than generate it since early blind individuals can make this symbol just as easily). These factors make it very likely that any normally developing psyche will make the circle = wholeness symbol association even if it has never encountered a mandala before.

8   The universe is like a tree. I will end this list of examples with one of the widest-spanning metaphors: the cosmic tree. How could this idea develop in the absence of specific cultural teaching? Simple: given our naturally emerging capacity for metaphor, it stands to reason that we will naturally tend to unconsciously picture similar ideas or associations as "connections" physically. A giant tree connects everything to everything else—and the same structure can be found in the idea of the "cosmic web" or the "cosmic rivers" found in so many mythologies. It's a fairly simple idea that makes a straightforward metaphor. The idea that everything is connected (in an interactional sort of way) to everything else can easily be depicted imagistically by a tree, or web, or sprawl of rivers, or any other thing that has lots of lines connecting the dots in a radial manner with everything coming from the center. Certainly there are cultural variations of this idea, but it seems to me that this imagery is immediately evident to the human organism due to all the underlying mental structure already there, both innate and self-taught. To claim that we are very unlikely to come up with this on our own without having been exposed to it before seems very hard to believe. Rather, I think because of the reasons given that we have a strong *natural tendency* to make this metaphor whenever we are contemplating the "big picture" or if life circumstances put us in a place where we are wondering about our "connection" to the rest of the world. This qualifies it as an archetype in exactly the way Jung defines it in his work—as an inborn tendency to make a particular kind of story or symbol structure—provided we amend "inborn" to "inborn and self-taught".

It should be obvious that we could multiply these examples into volumes. The point is merely that there is a large area in between the two options of unlearned-innate vs. culturally transmitted that are given in the discussion of archetypes. On the one end, there are psychological contents that emerge automatically without learning and on the other end are contents that are acquired because of some culturally-specific practice or idea that we imitate, observe in others or are directly taught. In between these categories is everything else: those symbols and images that are naturally prone to coalesce; they're easy to think and remember, and they "feel right" because of the way they connect our universal experiences with our unlearned human emotional predilections and our self-taught skills and symbolic associations. Moreover, many of these symbolic associations that later develop into full-blown metaphors start very early on while we were toddlers, and so they are implicit connections—i.e., they are in the unconscious.

Implications for archetype theory

This view helps us bridge the gap between unlearned, automatic contents and specifically learned, culturally passed-down contents that would not occur to you naturally had you not observed them or have them taught to you. The gap consists of psychological contents that do not come about automatically without learning, but neither do they have to be *culturally acquired*. They are contents which we all naturally teach ourselves about the world we live in with the body we have, which is why they can occur anywhere regardless of culture. So, how do we proceed from here with respect to archetype theory? What, if anything, should we concern ourselves with given the findings of genetics and early development? Do the findings of these disciplines really cast doubt on the foundational principles of analytical psychology?

In short: no, they don't. The reason is simple: Jung proposed that humans, by their nature, have a natural tendency to produce the same kinds of stories and symbols regardless of culture of origin. These stories can vary in detail but they won't vary in overall structure. Jung did not appear to require that these archetypes-as-such *must* be acquired without any environmental input whatsoever. Rather, he emphasized the *natural, non-culture-specific* human action in the environment. He used the far simpler analogy of the behavior of the leaf-cutter ant (Hogenson, 2009) to illustrate what he was getting at: that humans interact with their environment in a characteristically *human* way, and that way involves thinking a certain way and imagining in a certain way, much of which is self-initiated, self-organized and self-taught. By using this analogy and others like it, it seems Jung would have accepted universally self-taught contents under the archetypal umbrella.

Some of these elements will indeed require learning to develop—but that's not a problem for archetype theory so long as the *kind* of learning is universal *self-learning*. If Jung's idea was that every human has a repertoire of ready-to-make symbolic associations, from which arise archetypal images, I doubt if he would have quibbled or concerned himself with the idea that some of them involve universal self-learning. After all, even leaf-cutter ants teach themselves how to use their legs and mandibles; all animals do this kind of thing. In any case, this sort of self-learning happens universally due to the naturally occurring regularities of body, environment, emotion, and thought. These all form and create the foundational elements of the human imagination. The imagination, having all these innate and self-taught elements at its disposal, will then take our personal details and memories and break them down to create novel narratives in the form of dreams and visions, and it does so in accordance with symbolic associations that are readily available to every human. This is why they generate independently invented *forms* that nevertheless have differing *content*.

Mythic example: the sun god

Let's look at some of the associations I brought up above to see how they easily and unconsciously coalesce into mythic expressions. The sun is a good example. As we have seen, from very early on, we will all connect the sun with the circular shape, and we all feel its heat and observe its brilliant light as toddlers, as well as its position "up high". During the course of normal development, acting in concert with body-based sensations and a growing innate capacity for metaphor, these observations will naturally associate the sun's high position with power and "goodness", its heat with intense affect and with the feeling of "aliveness" (which it distributes everywhere), its light with knowledge. Finally, its circular shape lends itself as a fine symbol of wholeness. All that is left is personification—also universally occurring—to make the sun a deity, on high, associated with great knowledge, life, goodness, and wholeness. These connections all consist of links that we teach ourselves during our earliest years of life. They become part of implicit memory, and ripe for use during any time when spontaneous symbolic imagery is dominant in consciousness, such as dreaming or visionary experience. None of these associations, however, require any cultural input to make them—they occur naturally as a result of the extensive internally generated learning that occurs in early development, built upon the affective unlearned foundations we are born with.

Clinical example: alchemy dream

One more example. In therapy, a 45-year old female presented with this dream that she had right before therapy began:

> *I am going to the spa, or a gym, with my sister. We find a machine that is supposed to 'make us healthy'. We're not sure if we are allowed to use*

it, but we get on it anyway. Suddenly it encloses us in a black egg shaped apparatus and we start to tumble through it. It gets dark and progressively hotter through cycles, and my sister is panicking. Both of us tumble through in the fetal position. I reassure her that it will be ok, but I'm not sure it actually will end. Eventually it does, and it opens up. A manager is there to greet us.

Anyone familiar with the imagery of alchemical texts (see Eliade, 1974; Holmyard, 1990; and Jung, 1967, 1989a, 1993) will note many striking similarities between this dream and common themes found in the texts. For example, in many of these treatises and programs, the alchemist is shown or described engaging in the work with a "soror mystica" or a spiritual sister/divine guide or muse. The alchemist then blends the minerals in an egg shaped or spherical vessel that is very often likened to a womb. The working of the minerals is described as involving cyclical movement, turning, and also involves adding heat. The alchemical work must also be carried out in a specifically designed place set apart from the everyday. As mentioned, the work of alchemy is just as much a spiritual/psychological exercise as it is a physical transformation of minerals, and the alchemist is supposed to be at one with the materials she or he is working with. And finally, color symbolism plays a part also, in that the primordial substance, from which the end goal of the philosopher's stone or elixir of youth is created, is usually described as black—the *prima materia* as basic substance that everything is made of. Through the alchemist's work, the *prima materia* is transformed slowly and through many steps into the end goal: the philosopher's stone, or the Elixir of Youth, or the *aqua vitae*. With it the alchemist is supposedly able to achieve immortality and turn lead into gold.

Like the sun god above, here we can see this symbolism contains several examples of universally self-taught metaphorical associations: darkness/blackness = unknown, spinning = unsettling emotions, heat = intense affect, and the round (if not quite circular) shape of the "machine". This is to say nothing about the "fetal position" and "egg shape" of the machine which would be an obvious symbol of rebirth (note that the dreamer is literally tumbling through "in the fetal position"). To these, we add the personal details of the sister and the metaphor for going to therapy in "going to the gym to get healthy". As I hope is obvious by now, simply by developing in a characteristically human manner all of the above associations would be readily available to any human psyche based on the groundwork of symbolic associations we teach ourselves during early development, themselves based on innate processes. No familiarity with alchemical texts is needed because those same texts emerged from the same working human imagination operating as it normally does, creating metaphorical images of emotional situations.

Conclusions

So, what are we to make of this "third category" of self-taught contents? Does knowing that each of us, based on ubiquitous and non-culture-specific developmental events, self-organize a large array of symbolic associations and contents cast doubt upon Jung's theory of archetypes? That probably depends on how you read Jung. Jung did not have access to the body of developmental, neuroscientific, and ethological data that we have now. Having this knowledge now, he comes across as rather impressionistic and vague at times. For example, he states in his *Memories, Dreams, Reflections* that:

> The psyche of the child in its preconscious state is…already preformed in a recognizably individual way, and is moreover equipped with all specifically human instincts, as well as with the a priori foundations of the higher functions.
>
> Jung, 1989b: 348

Elsewhere, he states that, in regard to the development of archetypal imagery:

> We experience archetypal situations, that is, situations that humankind has experienced from time immemorial. These situations always repeat themselves, in various forms. We experience them as we have experienced them at all times.
>
> Jung & Meyer-Grass 2008: 162

And, in one of his last essays, he states that archetypes are

> an inherited *tendency* of the human mind to form representations of mythological motifs—representations that vary a great deal without losing their basic pattern.
>
> Jung, 1977: para 523

It seems to me that, given the apparently large array of contents that either emerge innately or are universally self-taught in early childhood, Jung's statements are entirely reasonable and very consistent with subsequent empirical research. It does not appear that he would have discounted self-taught contents at all in this analysis given these statements and many others like them, particularly because the very universality of self-taught contents would only lend *strength* to the idea that we have strong predispositions to make the associations found in independently invented symbolism. I also think this is true especially because none of this content requires very much in the way of imitative learning—that is, culture. Thus, to reframe Roesler's question, "are archetypes transmitted more by culture than biology?", I think the answer is, "no—they are transmitted primarily via a dense interaction between biology and universal, internally driven self-learning." In my mind, the evidence we have now shows that the human mind does indeed have a strong predisposition to make the associations found in catalogues of recurrent symbolism, just as Jung proposed, but this has little to do with cultural transmission. Rather, this is due to a combination of biological predispositions acted upon by intense internally directed but universally achieved learning, which is itself biologically based and continuously supported. As I see it, I don't think Jung could have hoped for any better confirmation of his theory.

References

Abboud, S., Maidenbaum, S., Dehaene, S., and Amedi, A. (2015). A number-form area in the blind. *Nature Communications*, 6: 6026. doi:10.1038/ncomms7026.

Alcaro, A., Carta, S., and Panksepp, J. (2017). The affective core of the self: A neuro-archetypical perspective on the foundations of human (and animal) subjectivity. *Frontiers in Psychology*, 8: 1424. doi:10.3389/fpsyg.2017.01424.

Bedny M., Pascual-Leone A., and Saxe R. (2009). Growing up blind does not change the neural bases of theory of mind. *Proceedings of the National Academy of Sciences of the United States of America*, 106(27): 11312–11317.

Bertolo, H., Paiva, T., Pessoa, L., Mestre, T., Marques, R. and Santos, R. (2003). Visual dream content, graphical representation and EEG alpha activity in congenitally blind subjects. *Cognitive Brain Research,* 15: 277–284.

Eliade, M. (1958). *Patterns in Comparative Religion.* London: Bison Press.

Eliade, M. (1974). *The Forge and the Crucible*, 2nd Ed. Chicago, IL: University of Chicago Press.

Gallagher, S. (2001). The practice of mind: Theory, Simulation or Interaction? In Evan Thomson (Ed.), *Between Ourselves: Second-Person Issues in the Study of Consciousness.* Cambridge, MA: Imprint Academic.

Goodwyn, E. (2012). *The Neurobiology of the Gods*. Princeton, NJ: Routledge.

Hogenson, G.B. (2009). Archetypes as action patterns. *Journal of Analytical Psychology*, 54: 325–337.

Holmyard, E.J. (1990). *Alchemy*. New York: Dover.

Jung, C.G. (1919). The structure and dynamics of the psyche. *The Collected Works of C.G. Jung, vol 8*. H. Read, M. Fordham, G. Adler and W. McGuire (Eds.), (trans. R.F.C. Hull). Routledge and Kegan Paul.

Jung, C.G. (1967). *Alchemical Studies. The Collected Works of C.G. Jung, vol 13*. H. Read, M. Fordham, G. Adler and W. McGuire (Eds.), (trans. R.F.C. Hull). Routledge and Kegan Paul.

Jung, C. G. (1977). *The Symbolic Life: miscellaneous writings. The Collected Works of C.G. Jung, vol 8*. H. Read, M. Fordham, G. Adler and W. McGuire (Eds.), (trans. R.F.C. Hull). Princeton, NJ: Princeton University Press.

Jung, C.G. (1989a). *Mysterium Coniunctionis. The Collected Works of C.G. Jung, vol 14*. H. Read, M. Fordham, G. Adler and W. McGuire (Eds.), (trans. R.F.C. Hull). Routledge and Kegan Paul.

Jung, C.G. (1989b). *Memories, Dreams, Reflections.* New York: Vintage.

Jung, C.G. (1993). *Psychology and Alchemy. The Collected Works of C.G. Jung, vol 12.* H. Read, M. Fordham, G. Adler and W. McGuire (Eds.), (trans. R.F.C. Hull). Routledge and Kegan Paul.

Jung, L. and Meyer-Grass, M (Eds.). (2008). *Children's Dreams: Notes from the Seminar Given in 1936–1940.* Princeton, NJ: Princeton University Press.

Karmiloff-Smith, A. (1992). *Beyond Modularity: A Developmental Perspective on Cognitive Science.* Boston, MA: MIT press.

Knox, J. (2003). *Archetype, Attachment, Analysis.* Hove: Brunner-Routledge.

Kövecses, Z. (1986). *Metaphors of Anger, Pride, and Love.* New York: John Benjamins.

Kupers, R. and Ptito, M. (2011). Insights from darkness: What the study of blindness has taught us about brain structure and function. *Progress in Brain Research,* 192:17–31. doi:10.1016/B978-0-444-53355-5.00002-6.

Kunz, M., Faltermeier, N. and Lautenbacher, S. (2012). Impact of visual learning on facial Expressions of physical distress: A study on voluntary and evoked expressions of pain in congenitally blind and sighted individuals. *Biological Psychology,* Feb 89(2):467–76. doi:10.1016/j.biopsycho.2011.12.016. Epub 2012 Jan 4.

Lakoff, G. and Johnson, M. (1998). *Philosophy in the Flesh.* New York: Basic Books.

Lakoff, G. and Turner, M. (1989). *More than Cool Reason.* Chicago: University of Chicago Press.

Lingnau, A., Strnad, L., He, C., Fabbri, S., Han, Z., Bi, Y., and Caramazza, A. (2014). Cross -modal plasticity preserves functional specialization in the posterior parietal cortex. *Cerebral Cortex,* 24: 541–549.

Mahon, B.Z., Anzellotti, S, Schwarzbach, J., Zampini, M., and Caramazza, A. (2009). Category-specific organization in the human brain does not require visual experience. *Neuron,* 63: 397–405.

Matsumoto, D. and Willingham, B. (2009). Spontaneous facial expressions of emotion of congenitally and noncongenitally blind individuals. *Journal of Personality and Social Psychology,* 96(1): 1–10.

McCune, L. (2010). Developing symbolic abilities. In B. Wagoner (Ed.), *Symbolic Transformation: The Mind in Movement Through Culture and Society* (pp. 173–192). London: Routledge Press.

Merchant, J. (2009). A reappraisal of classical archetype theory and its implications for theory and practice. *Journal of Analytical Psychology,* 54(3): 339–358.

Orr, E., and Geva, R. (2015). Symbolic play and language development. *Infant Behavior and Development* 38: 147–161.

Osório, A., Meins, E., Martins, C., Martins, E. C., and Soares, I. (2012). Child and mother mental-state talk in shared pretense as predictors of children's social symbolic play abilities at age 3. *Infant Behavior and Development* 35(4): 719–726.

Panksepp, J. (1998). *Affective Neuroscience: the Foundations of Human and Animal Emotions.* Oxford: Oxford University Press.

Panksepp, J. (2005). Affective Consciousness: Core Emotional Feelings in Animals and Humans. *Cognition and Consciousness,* 14: 30–80.

Pinker, S. (2007). *The Stuff of Thought.* New York: Viking.

Renier, L., De Volder, A.G., and Rauschecker, J.P. (2014). Cortical plasticity and preserved function in early blindness. *Neuroscience and Biobehavioral Reviews,* 41: 53–63.

Ricciardi E, Bonino D, Sani L, Vecchi T, Guazzelli M, Haxby J, Fadiga L, and Pietrini P. 2009. Do we really need vision? How blind people "see" the actions of others. *Journal of Neuroscience*, 29(31): 9719–9724.

Roesler, C. (2012). Are archetypes transmitted more by culture than biology? *Journal of Analytical Psychology*, 57: 224–247.

Saunders, P. and Skar, P. (2001). Archetypes, complexes and self-organization. *Journal of Analytical Psychology*, 46: 305–323.

Schinazi, V.R., Thrash, T., and Chebat, DR. (2016). Spatial navigation by congenitally blind individuals. *Wiley interdisciplinary reviews. Cognitive science*, 7: 37–58. doi:10.1002/wcs. 1375.

Sigalov, N., Maidenbaum, S., and Amedi, A. (2016). Reading in the dark: neural correlates and cross-modal plasticity for learning to read entire words without visual experience. *Neuropsychologia*, 83: 149–160.

Stevens, A. (2003). *The Archetype Revisited.* Toronto: Inner City Books.

Tinti, C., Adenzato, M., Tamietto, M., and Cornoldi, C. (2006). Visual experience is not necessary for efficient survey spatial cognition: Evidence from blindness. *The Quarterly Journal of Experimental Psychology*, 59(7): 1306–1328.

Tracy, J.L. and Matsumoto, D. (2008). The spontaneous expression of pride and shame: Evidence for biologically innate nonverbal displays. *Proceedings of the National Academy of Sciences of the United States of America*, 105(33): 11655–11660.

Chapter 3

On the origins of archetypes

Jon Mills

Erik Goodwyn (2020) provides a sophisticated critique of the nature versus nurture binary that has historically dogged archetype theory, hence showing this to be a false dichotomy, a topic I also deal with in depth (Mills, 2018, p. 201). Rather than privileging either innatism or empiricism as the origin and fulcrum of archetypal process, Goodwyn introduces a "third category," what I would call a mesotheory, that mediates between biological predisposition or nativism and cultural acquisition or internalization, which virtually makes such antipodal thinking obsolete. Nor does he strictly follow in the tradition of Jung, who vacillates in his speculations about the origins of archetypes coming from an innate collective psyche encompassing both organic ontic conditions and content derived from human experience encoded and imprinted on the deep structural configurations of the archaic mind. Contemporary Jungians have been more content in emphasizing one domain of the continuum over the other, such as evolutionary biology over socialization, emergence over apriorism, development over inheritance, and so forth, while Goodwyn seeks a middle ground. When it comes to the contents of archetypes, as he puts it, the question of "origins do not neatly fit into either category." Here he convincingly argues that when it comes to the transmission of archetypes, the biology versus culture duality is wrongly posed, for they are both operative in any discourse on archetypes, whether psychologically, symbolically, or transpersonally conceived.

The archetype-as-such and intermediacy

When Goodwyn discusses the archetype-as-such, he refers to Jung's postulate of the deeper inherited layer of the psyche as inborn structural proclivity while the content is often relegated to the appearance of images. This mirrors Jung's Kantian distinction between the noumenal *Ding an sich* and the mode of appearance, the world of the archetype *in itself* (as-such) versus the regulative, performative, and functional world of lived experience where the epistemological limit of knowing the supersensible is breached. Relying on Jung's (1947) insistence that the archetype possesses the "ability

DOI: 10.4324/9781003349921-3

to *organize* images and ideas" (p. 231; § 440) on the unconscious level, Goodwyn eschews the biology versus culture bifurcation, particularly arguing for how genetics *or* mere socialization cannot answer to such complexities. Rather, he evokes an intermediate domain where tendencies and action potentials "*arrange* memories and imaginary contents" belonging to "inherited archetypal structures." So, how does Goodwyn's position add to the archetype debate?

He specifically focuses on the archetype's tendency toward "*self-directed* learning" and this is what gives it its special character that is beyond the mere a priori embodied given, the impacts and effects of the lifeworld of personal experience, and the internalization of socialization processes such as language, culture, and symbolic transmission that originally transpire in early familial attachment and child development. But what seems to be missing from his discussion is any mention of agency, intentionality, or determinate (self-instituted) teleology inherent in the inborn capacity toward self-organization and purposeful self-expression that is implicit in such internally derived, directed, and self-taught learning that is fundamental to Goodwyn's thesis.

A mesotheory of the third

What does Goodwyn mean by a "third category" when positing archetypal process? He largely focuses on a "content source" that is self-initiated, "internally maintained and internally progressed," what I have previously attributed to "unconscious schemata," which are intrinsic organizing principles that are self-constituted and agentically executed (Mills, 2010). Rather than retain the binary discourse that has saturated analytical psychology, may I suggest this third category is more of a mediatory intervening function as a three-way relation to: (a) archaic ontology, namely, the corporeal, historical, and/or innate given of embodied biologic process; (b) our environmental surroundings in all their myriad forms, particulars, oppositions, and impositions as our being in the world; and (c) as self-relation to the experiential unfolding of interiority begotten within these other mediating dynamic domains. As relata, an archetype achieves a triadic or tertiary epigenetic level or emergent order of organization that serves mediatory functions. As an architectonic developmental agency enacted through and within the internal parameters and interposing external environs that inform its inner constitution and contours, an archetype is neither caused by evolutionary biology or genetics, nor is it the sole product of social development, environmental conditioning, or culture. Rather these complex forces are overdetermined and assimilated by archetypal agency. In effect, this third category is more like a performative and regulatory internal web of functional relations to self, other, and society within our natural encapsulated spacings in world that are ontically inseparable and systemically conjoined.

Goodwyn's *Third* as tertiary relation is really an intermediacy or meso-domain where mediation occurs. What he refers to as internally directed learning that is innately initiated and self-generated has been taken up extensively through the language of unconscious agency in my work (Cf. Mills, 2010, 2013b, 2018), yet his discussion of self-taught/self-directed learning could easily apply, as this is what is implied when attributing freedom, choice, and action to archetypes that are inborn a priori processes with self-derived impetuses and self-directed aims. When Goodwyn introduces the notion of the archetype-as-such as the "tendency to arrange" while omitting the most essential issue—namely, the question, scope, and limits of agency—this does not sufficiently explain, let alone shore up, the murky "third category" or intermediate emergence of mediatory relations that he likely wants to argue for.

If I understand him correctly, he wants to give priority to an unconscious a priori ground where we may situate and attribute some kind of unconscious agency to, whether personal or impersonal, which is informed by our evolutionary preconditions. This agentic function allows us to have self-derived, self-generated, self-directed tendencies toward broader and more sophisticated forms of self-organization we call psyche; and that input from our senses, or the experiential manifold of internalized objects in the world—environment, family, society, culture—allow us to form synthetic judgments independently from being taught them directly from others or through some passive or secondary process of mimesis. What develops is a sense of agency that makes self-learning possible; so it is not strictly biology or culture that is pushing the proverbial buttons, but an intermediary process of mediation that is a procreative self-instigated epigenetic achievement, which is internally commenced and linked to a fundamental unconscious subjectivity with degrees of innate freedom. In other words, this unconscious agency is the archetype-as-such, to use his preferred language.

Archetypal agency

The infrastructure of the brain is not the same as the Psyche, which is a higher order agency, a complex, self-determinative process system arising from its original dialectical autochthonous parameters. Although our embodiment is necessary and makes the experiential apparatus and internalization process possible, it is not a sufficient condition to explain psyche. Neither is our environmental facticity. What is missing from the equation is that intermediate mediatory sphere of the capacity to spontaneously express and actualize freedom in all its glory and shortcomings. This is where the language of archetypes intervenes nicely as a potential *explicans*. In other words, an archetype is self-constituted and self-generative within the context and confines of its immediate ontological thrownness.

Increasingly throughout his career Jung began to refer to archetypes as "autonomous" (*CW*, 9i, p. 40; *CW*, 11, p. 469), "autocratic," and manifesting themselves "involuntarily" to consciousness (*CW*, 9i, pp. 153–154, § 260), hence having a degree and level of independence emanating from the unconscious (see Mills, 2013a, for a review), which are "experienced as spontaneous entities" (*CW*, 8, p. 216) that "arise from self-creative acts" (Mills, 2018, p. 205). Following Jung, who attributes subjectivity to archetypes (see *CW*, 11, p. 469; *Letters II*, p. 22), if Goodwyn sees the archetype as a *psychic arranger*, much like the soul-animator that coordinates, controls, and directs the internal relations, forms, contents, and modes of unconscious process, then we may not inappropriately refer to this mediatory organizer as an unconscious nucleus or impersonal micro-agency spewing forth self-states into consciousness as the dispersal of its internal essence with quasi-autonomous properties bubbling up from within its deep abyss. What develops is a sense of agency or selfhood that makes further self-experience and self-learning possible. The content of such self-dispersal we have come to label and identify as manifestations of the archetypal. While the archetype-as-such is occluded, we experience and know its presence as appearances *within* consciousness.

Beyond the biology vs culture binary

Archetypes are beyond biology and culture for the simple fact that they elude the certainty of ground and beg the question of beginning. Because we cannot epistemologically discern their precise origins we are left to extrapolate from our inner experience of felt-causation, whether accurate, incorrect, or falsifiable. Inner experience does not necessarily mean truth, as we are accustomed to use the word, only disclosedness. What is made manifest to us must have a cause, a ground, a principle of sufficient reason that derives from origins, even if left indiscernible or undecidable. This is a logical proposition, not an experiential one, but the phenomenology of lived experience may simply be its own ground.

When pondering the question of origins, and in this context the source or genesis of archetypes, we must be humbled by an epistemological diffidence: we don't know. We don't even know if archetypes are *real*, other than employing a convention of language to signify some thing or designate some meaning to a nebulous abstract variable. We find ourselves embedded in the midst of being there (*Dasein*), of being *in* experience, even if an archetype is merely a metaphysical fiction. But when it comes to the metaphysics of experience, we are often seized by an inner presence that manifests itself from the unconscious, what we have come to call archetypal process. Where it comes from, that is, how it derives and arises, how it is organized, and how it expresses or relates to objects of experience through unconscious mediation is what we may abductively infer as the *pre-ontological*, namely, the preconditions of appearance as such, that is, *prior to beginning* and the manifestation of entities and objects of consciousness. But when it comes to the archetype-as-such, we are left with a speculative hypothesis of deducing original ground. Jung called this ground the collective unconscious or objective psyche, but this could very well be due to self-instantiating acts of self-generation derived from the archetype itself, a ground without a ground (*Ungrund*) that materializes from the autochthonous schematic organizations of immediate internal experience that makes the postulation of a collective unconscious—the hypostasis of soul—redundant (Mills, 2019).

This brings us back to a radicality of unconscious discourse that has become eclipsed by contemporary approaches in psychology that favor conscious experience over archaic ground or genesis. Although Goodwyn tends to dance around the issue of agency, intentionality, and the teleology of an archetype, his emphasis on the self-directed auto-learning of archetypal process adds another dimension to the unconscious dynamic structures of the psyche we should seriously consider in this ongoing debate.

References

Goodwyn, E.D. (2020). Archetypal origins: Biology vs culture is a false dichotomy. *International Journal of Jungian Studies*, 13(2): 111–129. doi:10.1163/19409060-bja10002

Jung, C.G. (1953–1977). *Collected Works of C.G. Jung*; Bollingen Series, 20 vols. Eds. H. Read, M. Fordham, G. Adler; (Trans. R.F.C. Hull). London: Routledge & Kegan Paul; Princeton: Princeton University Press. (Hereafter referred to *CW* by vol. no.)

Jung, C.G. (1934/1954). Archetypes of the Collective Unconscious. *CW*, 9, pt.1: pp. 3–41.

Jung, C.G. (1940). The Psychology of the Child Archetype. *CW*, 9, pt.1: pp. 151–181.

Jung, C.G. (1947). On the Nature of the Psyche. *CW*, 8: pp. 159–234.

Jung, C.G. (1951/1973–1975). *Letters of C.G. Jung. Vol. II: 1951-1961.* London: Routledge and Kegan Paul.

Jung, C.G. (1952). Answer to Job. *CW*, 11: pp. 355–470.

Mills, J. (2010). *Origins: On the Genesis of Psychic Reality*. Montreal: McGill-Queens University Press.

Mills, J. (2013a). Jung's metaphysics. *International Journal of Jungian Studies*, 5(1), 19–43.

Mills, J. (2013b). Freedom and determinism. *The Humanistic Psychologist* 41(2), 101–118.

Mills, J. (2018). The essence of archetypes. *International Journal of Jungian Studies* 10(3), 199–220.

Mills, J. (2019). The myth of the collective unconscious. *Journal of the History of the Behavioral Sciences* 55: 40–53.

Chapter 4

Commentary on Mills' "The essence of archetypes"

Erik Goodwyn

Introduction

In philosopher and psychoanalyst Jon Mills' essay "The Essence of Archetypes" (2018), the author takes an approach that examines the concept of the archetype merely in terms of what must occur for an archetypal image to emerge in consciousness, without reference to neuroscience or biology, but rather on a purely experiential level. That is, Mills seeks to understand what essential characteristics the archetype-as-such must have in order to give rise to archetypal images/experiences, but he remains entirely in the intrapsychic realm so as not to muddy the waters with any discussion of first substance which he feels is epistemologically messy.

This maneuver is simultaneously the greatest strength of Mills' approach and, in my opinion, its only weakness. Overall, I find Mills' treatment to be unique and insightful, providing a new set of conceptual tools with which to understand the archetype in terms of its internal dynamics and consistent qualities. In so doing, Mills refuses to engage in any discussion about what (if any) biological or other contributions there may be to the archetype. This creates a discourse that has a certain purity to it that has a kind of mathematical precision I think is very valuable because he shows in a powerful and logical way that such concerns are actually unnecessary to demonstrate the *necessity* of the concept of archetype no matter what sort of metaphysics one employs. But regardless of this great strength of approach, the fact remains that we humans *are* enmattered beings, and the matter of which we are composed (or equivalent to, or whatever depending on your metaphysics) has certain regularities to it as given to us by the observations of the biological sciences. So, refusing to engage with this question as such will only give us *part* of the answer to the question of archetypal origins. That said, Mills' treatment is so thorough and so powerful, any of us who is willing and able to approach the subject now has a set of potent, well thought-out tools to use to attempt a comparison of the sort he understandably avoids.

Thus, I remain unconvinced, at least at this point, that we can *fully* discuss archetypal origins without some kind of metaphysics of mind lurking

DOI: 10.4324/9781003349921-4

in the background, even if it is not specifically stated, or, as in here, even if it is deliberately avoided. What is most impressive about this essay, though, is that it retains so much power anyway, provided we stay within the boundaries Mills himself has set for us. That said, there are a few times where it seems he strays from these boundaries and reveals an unstated position on the subject, before he returns again to his primary charge. At such times, I think he detracts unnecessarily from his main objective.

Explanations and boundaries of explanations

For example, Mills states that my own argument that archetypes are attractor states in the narrative field created by innate mental biases and constraints (Goodwyn, 2013) "could just as easily be explained through psychodynamic motivations based in unconscious desire, defense, and identification." This objection contains two problems. First is that this is simply an assertion without any supporting detailed explanation to back it up. If indeed it could just as easy be explained as such, then let's hear it so that we can evaluate its plausibility. None of the attractor states I discuss in my 2013 article is provided with a counter-example using these explanatory parameters. And even if such a counter-example were given, the next step would still need to be taken: that of providing us with evidence from the literature that those examples were indeed plausibly responsible for such attractor states, rather than just *possible* explanations. Any set of affairs could *possibly* be explained a number of ways. Evidence, however, helps us narrow down which ones are most plausible. Mills regrettably does not provide us with any, though in fairness it is not his primary objective anyway.

The second problem is that it is not immediately obvious that these two types of explanation are mutually exclusive anyway. Just how do unconscious desires, defenses, and identifications relate to innate, biologically based mental biases and constraints? To answer that question, one needs some kind of metaphysics of mind that provides us with how the game is played—that is, how mind relates to matter. Where, for example, do unconscious desire, defense, and identification come from, if they are not emergent from evolutionary and biological precursors? Without clearly delineating that these two explanatory frameworks are indeed mutually exclusive, we cannot dismiss the first framework by saying "it could explained by" the second framework, because I can similarly say the second framework "could be" explained using my first. We will see a few more examples of this sort of quibble below.

The characteristics of the archetype

Mills' proposal is that archetypes are, and indeed *must be* unconscious, universal, self-propagating, initially formless and featureless essences that *generate* basic form and hence direct the acquisition and organization of mental content. From there archetypal images manifest in multiple particulars, appearing in an overdetermined fashion in various cultural expressions that nevertheless have universal origins. This proposal is presented as a brute fact of psychic life, but a necessary one that *must* exist in order to account for the psychic origin of any repeating, universal content (the evidence of which is abundant). For Mills, empirical demonstrations of the existence of archetypes are not necessary, since using no more than the principle of sufficient reason alone, he argues that it logically follows that archetypes *must* exist. Thus, it is no more necessary to "prove" archetypes exist than it is to "prove" that 2 + 2 = 4. As mentioned before, of course, the proposal that these processes are brute facts, however, is where he stops. That is, Mills is intensely interested in *phenomenological origins* but does not task himself with sketching out why psyche might have such universal essences in the first place and what *their* origin is, presumably because such questions might draw us into questions of first substance, or tempt us to make crass biological (or other) reductive errors.

Mills proposes that the archetype is the source "from which phenomena manifest, namely, that which conditions all experience." In this sense, Mills appears to presuppose a kind of intrapsychic Aristotelian foundationalism—i.e., that there is some sort of ground of (psychic) being rather than infinitism or circular dependence. In other words, Mills seems to advocate that phenomenal experience itself has an underlying structure wherein there is a ground of psychic being from which experiential content derives, and this ground is the *ultimate* ground rather than itself derivable from something prior or from some posterior product of itself, though as mentioned before, Mills remains agnostic as to how this ground is or is not related to the concept of physical matter. Given that he is using the principle of sufficient reason, this foundationalism is entirely reasonable.

In the next section, titled "on essence" Mills sets out to describe the various processes that the essence of the archetype must undergo in order to manifest in phenomenal experience: first of all, the primordial unity of which all archetypes participate must undergo a basic fractionation, at which point the archetype is no longer simple and undivided. The rest of the process must follow a basic course: going from simple unity, to division into identity and difference, through its particular presubjective impersonal formalism which entails a basic teleological directedness. This leads us to the concept of archetypal agency, though we will return to the processual changes later.

Archetypes, agency, and the transpersonal

At this point we diverge again from the boundaries previously set up before, and Mills criticizes Jung's more unabashedly poetic descriptions of archetypes as presenting themselves like gods, claiming it is absurd to contemplate it in this manner and "should not be equated with personal entities, let alone deified presences, floating about in the psyche and casting a spell on the individual like a voodoo incantation." Despite this warning, he nevertheless goes on to describe archetypes as unconscious schemata which are freely determined, "self-constituted and determinate within the natural parameters in which they find themselves and operate...unconscious agency ultimately underlies the constitution of all mental functioning." Later, he argues that though the archetype is not "strictly speaking" a personality or agent, it nevertheless has an inherent teleology that exudes and executes agency with independence, self-assertion, and the capacity for self-manifestation, that is deriving from an "unconscious organizing principle that is internally impelled to materialize." This means that archetypes have "an agentic character" with an autonomous quality, self-derived and self-activating. With these passages it seems that Mills is criticizing Jung and yet confirming his intuitions at the same time. He appears to quibble with Jung over whether or not to strictly label archetypes as actual personalities or agents—and it seems doubtful that Jung would have gone quite that far—to then nevertheless agree with him on the *characteristics* that the archetype has that suggest such an analogy. To say that an archetype is an independent, agentic, organizing principle with inherent teleology, self-assertion, self-manifestation, and then to criticize Jung's occasional depiction of them as godlike powers in the mind seems to me to be an objection to the sometimes flowery way Jung describes them rather than any real disagreement in concept itself.

Similarly Mills criticizes language that speaks of archetypes as having a "transpersonal" origin, equating such speculation to "conjuring up a supernatural macroanthropos." Obviously finding such an idea objectionable influences his decision to demand that all of this occurs "from within," in order to avoid "those claiming, as Jung did, that archetypes are transpersonal, cosmic external occurrences or organizations superimposed on our interior [that] have a messy epistemological burden to reckon with." Taking the purely experiential approach presupposes that such things cannot be proven or disproven and so speak entirely of how everything is going on "from within." But, within what? Unless we are willing to begin classifying substances as within or without—a maneuver Mills is trying to avoid—the best we can do is to label some experiences as having a quality of *apparent interiority* and others as not having this quality. Such experiences may or may not fall under the categories of transpersonal or even supernatural (whatever that may mean), but without a metaphysics of mind from which to operate, we can neither criticize nor confirm such a framework. Otherwise engaging the concepts and categories here is only to invite the "messy epistemological burden" and tackle it head on.

The emergence of archetypal derivatives

In any case, the next section describes the sequence of events leading to the emergence of an archetypal image. This section is, I think, the most powerful part of Mills' analysis, because it gets right at the heart of what an archetype appears to really do. The process plays out according to Mills as: the archetype begins in inchoate form, then self-organizes via first delineating a boundary between self and non-self. Then, through continued cycles of self-reflection, it further develops progressively more differentiated capacities for apperception and differentiation, all fueled by an internally detected *lack* which gives it directedness. This lack appears as a "desire to wake, to apprehend itself, to manifest, is the expression of its own felt-being in relation to lack. This is the prototype of the human psyche." This elegant passage helps to further describe the most basic structural experiential constitution of an archetype, and describing it as a prototype of the psyche helps us to see the psyche's fractal nature as well. At the level of consciousness, which is also a manifestation of the same sort of process and archetypal in its own right, we have the previously described "birth of an archetype," which will be apprehended by the conscious ego, and in the manner of a nested hierarchy.

This sequence established, we take another unnecessary side-journey. Here he states, again opposing any talk of archetypes as coming from "without," that archetypes "feel like they are connected to something outside of or independent from the self despite that fact that they arise from and are encountered within." He argues, rather, that the appearance of such an autonomous event as uncanny and numinous but that the experience of it as "alien" or maximally "other" is a mistake and delusion. But, how can we say this if we refuse to lay the groundwork for what "within" and "without" mean? Again, this diversion seems to detract from his overall vision and does not add much to what he is developing.

To recognize it as non-other but nevertheless quintessentially emerging from "within" is to blend two things which are, in fact, distinct. By that I mean only that we cannot fuss about whether or not archetypes *really* come from "without," even though they may feel like they do, until we are much more clear about what "within" and "without" actually mean. The problem here seems to be tangled into the question of which is more fundamental: ontology or epistemology. I do not intend to try to resolve that debate here—I only mean to point out that the question of what exactly the nature of the boundary between mind and whatever else there might be out there is one with many answers. Just within the field of philosophy of mind, for example, a number of frameworks exist that do not require any hard boundary between mind and matter. Among these include idealist monism, dual-aspect monism, and neutral monism (I explore this issue in more detail in Goodwyn, 2019). None of these frameworks require archetypes to be considered mysterious transcendent entities pulling the psychic strings from a mysterious unknowable realm. At the same time, however, such psychic forces do not in any recognizable way come from "within" in the sense Mills appears to be using here—i.e., emerging entirely within the piece of psyche I call my own. This is because the very term "individual psyche" loses much of its punch in such monistic systems: rather than cleanly isolated psyches emerging from some non-mental ground state via some as-yet unknown mechanism, the monistic ontologies above assume that individual psyches are merely local aspects of a much bigger unified substance—metaphorically speaking, in such a system we would more accurately viewed not as planets floating in the void, each utterly self-contained and separate from others, but islands, the tips of which are seen—rightly so—as separate, but with the knowledge that this separateness is undergirded by a less visible (but no less real) interconnectedness. Each ego is the island, but it is built out of the continuous terrain under the ocean.

In this latter sense, archetypes are both "external"—since they do not emerge from within the individual island of psyche—and yet still do not have to be seen as coming from some purely abstractified and illegitimately mysterious "realm," which Mills correctly identifies is nearly impossible to justify on epistemological grounds. And yet, neither do we have to claim that archetypes originate solely within the individual psyche either—a proposition not only do I think Jung would have objected to, but is nevertheless incoherent within a dual-aspect or neutral monist model anyway; in such a metaphysics of mind, there really is no such thing as a wholly individual psyche—only wholly individual egos, each built upon successive layers of progressively more universal and impersonal substrata, at the origin of which is the "neutral substance."

Do any of these complaints necessarily contradict Mills' formulation of archetype? Not really, though it does provide a deeper context behind the processes he identifies, as it gives us a more clear sense of what is meant by the word "intrapsychic": "within" the subjective and qualitatively "interior" experience of a conscious ego, but otherwise not *actually* separate from the rest of the universe in a rigid categorical manner, but rather separate only in the degree of conscious awareness and/or in connection with personal identity and selfhood.

The one and the many

Continuing on, Mills describes the archetype as originating in an initial split in a "solipsistic" unity, and these archetypes are utilized by the mind as a means of conferring meaning and grounding ourselves:

> Just as an archetype discovers itself in its otherness, the Other is its externalization from sameness and lost unity. In its otherness, it wants to return to itself, its lost immediacy, yet at the same time seeks the

universal in its differentiation....The breaking up of initial unity is tantamount to the cosmogonic act of dispersing its essence into the world....Psychic activity rests on a fulcrum of difference and negation to the degree that without an identifiable and discernable Other, any notion of the archaic would be tantamount to simplicity and solipsism, an untenable proposition in our pluralistic world of particularity and contextual difference.

Mills concedes that archetypes are registered, perceived, and felt by the psyche, but feels that considering them to be independent of mind and culture to be unlikely. Yes, from an epistemological, categorical, and phenomenological point of view, they present themselves as autonomous forces in the psyche, but Mills feels we cannot know their metaphysical status. Invoking Platonic forms, as Jung does, Mills feels is unverifiable. In this vein, he criticizes the idea of the transcendent function seeking wholeness as "a logical fallacy and a fantasy the psyche manufactures in its pursuit of wholeness." Unfortunately we are given no rationale to lead us to this rather startling conclusion—that the pursuit of wholeness is either an infantile desire or an imaginary concept.

This final side-journey is even more challenging to grasp as we continue, since later, Mills calls the transcendent function a "regathering of the original split in unity synthesized through our reflective acts of apprehending otherness...The Other is the supersession of the original unity as particularized plurality only to participate within the One, the encompassing universality that pervades psyche and culture. As archetype disperses its essence into multiplicity, it becomes other to itself, only to recover its original lost unity in such otherness as a return to itself."

This passage encapsulates the transcendent function wonderfully, but as I hope is clear by now, the presentation of it as an alternative to Jung's description of the process has the same issue that the discussion of archetype as "external" to the psyche has: namely, a conceptual tangle that is dependent upon our underlying metaphysical assumptions about the nature of what psyche actually is. If we are going to remain agnostic on this question, as Mills purports to do, then Platonic Forms, mind- or culture-independent origins, and natural pulls toward wholeness are all just as likely as unlikely to be real. Hence, it seems Mills *wants* to be agnostic but then takes a stand on the subject anyway without expressly stating what it is. After all, if we're not going to talk about what sort of substance psyche is or is not, and we're going to propose that archetypes are simply brute facts of psyche—and there are very good reasons for adopting this agnosticism—then criticizing Platonic Forms or the idea of transcendent unity makes little sense. You have to take a position on what sort of thing psyche *is* first and justify it before you can then subsequently explain why such things are unreal, incoherent, or implausible. Mills only does half the work needed here to make such claims.

Conclusion

It might seem that I generally am being very critical of Mills' essay—this would be a mistake to assume, however. In general, I think this contribution is very important and helps to clarify and highlight a number of issues regarding archetype theory that have gone undiscussed. My observations are merely quibbles, and those quibbles, as one can see, require quite a bit of setup to explain why they concern me at all. But I don't want these quibbles to detract from the overall quality of Mills' work, which I feel is extremely high.

In fact, the strength of Mills' approach is that it provides a clear, straight-forward way to describe how archetypes manifest in phenomenal experience at the most fundamental structural level. But I think the limitations placed on the approach do not really escape the metaphysical issues in the hoped-for way in every instance. Even using language such as "within" and "external" and so forth presuppose an unspoken, dimly characterized relationship between mind and matter that colors the subsequent discussion and forces us into the assessment of archetypal autonomy, origins, agency, etc. that is given. Without really working through the possibilities, it is assumed that the division between internal and external are clear and distinct, and anything thence labeled "external," furthermore, is highly suspect, either as an epistemologically questionable proposition, or as a pure flight of super-stitious fantasy, for which Mills seems to have great skepticism for, if not outright contempt.

But as I said, these complaints I have about the analysis only apply when Mills' appears to step outside of the epistemological boundaries he has set up for himself at the outset. When he remains firmly within them, which he indeed does through the majority of the essay, his analysis is in my opinion indisputable, elegant, and nuanced. If I had any other wish, it would be to fix the relative lack of specific discussion of how all this might play out in the case of a particular archetype. Rather, the discussion is kept almost entirely in the abstract—so much, so, in fact, that it runs the risk of losing sight of what we really mean by "archetype"—that is, the original phenomena which drew Jung to speaking of archetypes in the first place—cross-cultural symbols. Such cross-cultural symbols are never mentioned except in the ab-stract. But again, that is another minor quibble.

In any case, I agree with the rationale behind the conceptual caution be-hind the decision to steer clear of the metaphysics of mind and any discus-sion about biology or evolutionary science. And, in fact, if Mills had not in my opinion drifted outside of that boundary here and there, and only in terms of concepts and never in terms of biological science, I would have little to complain about. That said, I (obviously) believe that it is possible to dis-cuss psyche in tandem with biological science and metaphysics of mind *with-out* making grievous category errors or crass reductions. The requirement, however, is that in order to do so one must make a stand on the Mind–Body Problem, whether explicitly stated, or (as is unfortunately often the case) implicitly assumed presupposition. Mills refuses to take any stance on what the substantive relation between mind and matter might be; unfortunately, in some ways this does not get him out of the game. To take no stance, but then to speak freely of "within" and "without" when referring to psyche, already rules out some of the contenders in the running.

This is easily fixed by simply avoiding such language at the outset. But even with all that said, what is truly remarkable about Mills' work is that doing so detracts really nothing from his overall analysis. In the end, Mills does what he sets out to do: shows that archetypes must exist, describes in rigorous terms the essence of what all archetypes must be, and how they self-organize in our lived experience.

Reference

Goodwyn, E. (2019). Jung and the mind body problem. In J. Mills (Ed.), *Jung and Philosophy*. Princeton, NJ: Routledge.

Chapter 5

Archetypal metaphysics and the psyworld

Jon Mills

I am grateful to Erik Goodwyn (2020b) for his perspicacious critique of my essay on the essence of archetypes (Mills, 2018) and his penetrating analysis that identifies contradictions, gaps, and unaddressed issues I remain silent on in that work. His critique challenges me to further hone my thinking on the philosophical parameters of an archetype in response to his pointed questions and queries in relation to his own contributions on innateness (Goodwyn, 2010), the origins of archetypes as attractor states that are biologically constituted (Goodwyn, 2013), his recent scholarship on the mind–body problem in Jung (Goodwyn, 2019), as well as his sophisticated argument of how an archetype is internally self-directed (Goodwyn, 2020a), what I believe offers a new mesotheory of agentic mediation (Mills, 2020a).

Goodwyn's gracious engagement of my text offers many inquiries and reservations that merit a meticulous response and further elaboration. His main criticism is that I do not engage the conventional discourse on archetypes from the standpoint of neuroscience and biology nor as arising from culture, but rather I stay of the purely experiential level on how an archetype appears in consciousness. He specifically charges that I do not discuss nor take a stand on the question of first principles, or what he refers to as "first substance," and that I refuse to engage any discussion of biological or other factors contributing to the essence and origins of an archetype, what he both admires for my methodology yet also decries is lacking a formal metaphysics. I will address his concerns in turn before offering my own views on the ontology of an archetype that have direct bearing on a metaphysics of mind. What I hope to do is sketch out a preliminary framework for an archetypal metaphysics that introduces the notion of *psyworld*, which may be seen as an intercessor between embodiment and experience.

Embodiment

Professor Goodwyn rightfully reminds us that we are enmattered, and the matter of which we are composed of is subject to observation and investigation by the biological sciences. I emphatically agree. We are embodied

DOI: 10.4324/9781003349921-5

beings and this is an ontological given, the details of which are arguable, as he notes, just as his recognition that this issue was not the focus of my essay. But, we are on the same page. Our embodiment is a necessary condition for an archetype to emerge, but it is not necessarily a sufficient one to explain the complexifications and ontic dynamic organizations inherent in archetypal process and their emergence. Having said that, Goodwyn is interested in knowing what kind of metaphysics of mind is "lurking in the background" behind the appearances I try to delineate as archetypal manifestations. Rightfully so. Before I attempt an adumbrated answer, let me say that the very question can be approached from many vantage points, all with varying benefits, disadvantages, and propositional assumptions that must be clarified. Should we assume the Kantian phenomenal–noumenal dualism Jung often evokes? Could we explain this from the standpoint of some monism, particularly dual-aspect or neutral monism or some variation? What about presentism—only present things exist? I have argued that essence must appear in order for anything to be real, including an archetype. But we may also consider the Heideggerian move that dis-closedness is both revealed and hidden, unveiled yet concealed, uncovered yet occluded. Of course, we are thrown into embodiment—the material world, our physical bodies, culture, language, cosmos—only the modes of Being and minutia of appearances are varied. The metaphysical quibbles are endless.

Goodwyn wants to bring us back to the naturalized question of physicalism and scientific realism. I must admit that early in my career, I was concerned about the bane of material reduction (Mills, 2002), but later came to the conclusion that naturalized accounts of mind do not necessarily devolve into a crass positivist framework or misguided scientism based upon how we conceive of matter and energy. I certainly do not ascribe to the notion of immateriality or the existence of entities that have no form or substance, be it only thought or thinking itself, which, of course, must arise within our embodiment, just as the energetic stratification of matter must inhere or ingress in something in order to manifest, hence be real. And given that the field of physics has adopted the scope and language of metaphysics, and particularly a philosophy of containment *and* concealment (such as dark matter/energy), there is much compatibility, the pragmatics and details of which I do not need to defend here. Before offering a proposed metaphysics (please be patient), let me prepare the ground so that Goodwyn's concerns are addressed more explicitly.

Attractor states and boundaries of explanation

Goodwyn rightfully accuses me of slipping in a non sequitur when I summarize his thesis that archetypes are attractor states that could be explained through unconscious psychodynamic motivations and constraints without providing a detailed argument or evidence to back up my assertion with plausibility. What I had in mind with regards to the organization and dynamics of attractor states is related to my commentary on his recent essay on archetypal origins and the question of agency (Mills, 2020a). In complementing his theory (Goodwyn, 2013), attractor states could be viewed as agentic processes within unconscious schemata or the archetype itself. Let us speculate that the phenomena of attractor states seek out objects to mate with and incorporate into their own internal structure, biological or otherwise. Therefore the complex ongoing self-organization of an archetype as a process system (a) desires and aims toward engaging and absorbing objects via its experiential field; and (b) it may further form defensive organizations against objects of experience, so we may potentially see detractor states that equally repel against objects due to perceived threats that could endanger the integrity of the archetype if the object were incorporated or merged. This desirous-defensive process system also forms a rudimentary pole of opposition in the archetype, which must mirror a much more complex order within Psyche itself as a web of inner contradictions reflective of the robust compendium of varieties of oppositions (Mills, 2019b), such as the coincidence of opposites (*coincidentia oppositorum*) and their complexity (*complexio oppositorum*), hence giving rise to complementarity, tensions, conflicts, compensation, and their conjunction (*coniunctio oppositorum*), ultimately leading toward their union through the transcendent function.[1]

Goodwyn asks "how do unconscious desires, defenses, and identifications relate to innate, biologically based mental biases and constraints?" Here, he believes to answer this question one needs a metaphysics of mind to make sense of it all, and particularly "how mind relates to matter." I am not disputing his claim, the details of which we may very well leave to others to define, explain, and cavil about, but with a caveat that just because we are embodied does not mean we are nothing but physical processes in the brain informed by evolutionary pressures, as we are complex systems that undergo their own epigenetic achievements and developmental evolutions within their own process of becoming. Where do unconscious desire, defense, and identification come from?, he asks. I would say, they come from the archetype itself as a self-organized teleological agency; but on a more fundamental level, we could attribute this to drives (*Triebe*) or our embodied existence in which we are thrown, which gives rise to internal organic expansions, such as sentience, biologically based urges, affect, and pulsions seeking objects for satisfaction, assimilation, fusion, and so forth. This is how a drive operates: it has a source, telos, aim, and object with innate, built-in (organic, evolutionary) capacities for impetus, desire (biases), and motivational constraints (defenses, compromise formations, etc.). The more complex the system becomes, the more variation in quantitative and qualitative functions are enacted and observed; but the complex system must also derive from a fundamental constituent or essence that comprises the basic units of mental life. So, just as the complexity of psyche emerges from its ontic epigenetic origins, so must an archetype exhibit a core organizational structure or form that participates in this larger developmental process of becoming. This is what I refer to as an unconscious schema.

While professor Goodwyn does an excellent job of highlighting and delineating their material-efficient causality, I am more concerned with the formal-final causal processes of an archetype. To be sure, all causal processes are operative at any given time in an intricate multifaceted system with some features being emphasized over others based on the level and range of their complexity, valence, intensity, and form. This accounts for multiple plains of explanation depending upon what component of a system is being analyzed at any given moment and avoids committing a mereological fallacy where higher architectonic organizations and epiphenomenal features are boiled down to an original substance that strips the archetype of autonomy and freedom, which attractor states should be able to account for in theory.

On ground and universal essence

The brute fact of psychic existence is that we find ourselves as given, as being here, as living presence ontologically thrown into a body, a material *and* mental world, family, community, culture, language, and so forth, that which we confront and are confronted with, one purpose of which is to encounter (on ontological/ontic and existential/existentiell levels) and assimilate into our burgeoning psychic realities. This is our constitutional historicity that is part of fundamental ontology, or what I call archaic primacy, and experientially bestowed a priori, the onto-structural conditions in which we find ourselves. This, of course, is to assume a form of critical or scientific realism: namely, that the physical universe and the human world precedes our individual (particular) existence, which we find ourselves in and alongside the multiplicity of Being. Goodwyn's main concern is that I do not go far enough and address the question of "first substance." He asks us "why psyche might have such universal essences in the first place and what *their* origin is?" These are indeed difficult questions to sustain.

The issue of ground—whether it be foundationalism, coherentism, infinitism, circular (or dialectical) dependence, absolutism, or in the onto-theological/transcendentalist tradition, a ground without a ground (*Ungrund*)—simultaneously engages the question of essence regardless of where we want to locate its ultimate source or discourse. Since the linguistic turn, these debates typically rest on epistemological assumptions and definitional disputes dislocated from their original historical contexts. Depending upon how we define these terms, we will get different propositional attitudes, suppositions, and significations. Are there non-repeating finite chains, repeating finite chains, non-repeating infinite chains, repeating infinite chains, infinite finite chains, or finite infinite chains? Is there a beginning and/or end to infinity? If essence must appear in order for any-thing to be real, then it has to come from somewhere: it does not just pop up *ex nihilo*. Does it come from itself, a prior ontology (even pre-ontological), or from a posterior position in which it arises from within in its own imme-diacy? These questions beg the origin of origins, of which we may hopelessly fall into an infinite regress or simply remain agnostic about.

Goodwyn is wanting an answer to the question of ground and its rela-tion to "the concept of physical matter." He himself has discussed the hard problem of neuroscience in addressing these matters with regard to the mind–body problem, so he is well aware of the lure and dangers of phys-ical reduction and how it does not resolve the question of consciousness. Instead, he advocates for a Neoplatonic neutral monism where there is a unitary wholeness to the universe that ontologically exists prior to all par-ticularization (and presumably participation), or parts from which all is derived (Goodwyn, 2019, pp. 80–81). In other words, all entities and appear-ances arise from a first substance, the wholeness of the cosmos, the *Unus Mundus*, hence a holistic monism, rather than the notion that holism is a developmental achievement that arises out of its earlier constituencies. For Goodwyn, the whole is not derived from parts nor is it merely the sum of its parts: it is the metaphysical ground from whence all arises.

Preliminary considerations toward an archetypal metaphysics

In positing the whole before the part, the universal before the particular, the One before the many, we have entered into the domain of speculative metaphysics with a number of potential outcomes and sundry problemat-ics. It is for this reason that I adopt a two-fold approach in order to ob-viate (and hence avoid answering) these knotty issues: (1) I start with a phenomenological-ontic description of the unfolding of interiority, or what is experienced from the "inside"—which Goodwyn has a problem with—rather than the standpoint of the "outside;" and (2) I develop a theoretical paradigm of the archetype as emerging from a developmental monistic on-tology. Let me explain.

The methodological position I begin with in my investigation of the es-sence and appearance of an archetype is what I call *onto-phenomenology* or *internal ontology*. I am interested in tracing the steps of internally derived experience. If an archetype exists, it must have an (a) internal self-structure that (b) materializes in some form, or it would not be actual. I am starting from this perspective. But even if you start with phenomenology, you must have an ontological condition or ground from which the organization and experience of phenomenon comes from, occurs, and appears. This is tied to its earliest (archaic) structural conditions that inform how phenomena manifest regardless of how we define or describe them to be. If emergence or manifestation begins from more simple configurations and then advances in organizational complexity and content within unique contingencies and contexts in which it finds itself budding, then you have a developmental monism that connects the most primordial, unrefined, and rudimentary (often organic structures) to the more sophisticated evolving shapes over time that further build on its maturational, epigenetic achievements, which it absorbs into its internal configurations as a more robust whole. That is the basic framework, but we could make it very elaborate depending upon where we want to go with it. My basic aim here is to articulate how internally derived agency expresses itself through fractionation as the manifestation of teleology, which is the externalization of its essence: in other words, the *presence of essence*.

Goodwyn ups the ante and says that because I attribute autonomy, agency, and self-directed teleology that are part of an archetype's organizational principles that then self-manifest, I really should not be critical of Jung when he dips into language that seems to attribute "godlike powers" to an archetype. But the difference here is crucial: unlike the concept of God, archetypes are not self-caused. Although they are autopoietic, they are not created *ex nihilo* from omnipotence (or from any omniproperties) or pure thought thinking itself into existence or thinking about its operations of being and becoming. I rather prefer to view archetypes as arising from within their natural parameters, of which Goodwyn would relegate to biological systems operating within the archetype itself. But, what I would suggest is that we can have many strata of *explanandum* as we can have many *explanans*. We do not need to collapse origin into its material substratum to make the case that an archetype is much more than that, just as Goodwyn proposes in his own theory that weds biology and culture into its own ontological mosaic.

My use of conventional language such as "within," "interiority," and "externality" is something of a sticking point for Goodwyn (2020b), especially when I question transpersonal (hence supernatural) presuppositions:

> Taking the purely experiential approach presupposes that such things cannot be proven or disproven and so speak entirely of how everything is going on "from within." But within what? Unless we are willing to begin classifying substances as within or without—a maneuver Mills is trying to avoid—the best we can do is to label some experiences as having a quality of *apparent interiority* and others as not having this quality. Those that do not may or may not fall under the categories of transpersonal or even supernatural (whatever that may mean), but without a metaphysics of mind from which they operate, we can neither criticize nor confirm such a framework. Otherwise engaging the concepts and categories here, is only to invite the "messy epistemological burden" and tackle it head on.

In evoking the need to take a stand on a "metaphysics of mind" operating within the qualia of experience, he is suggesting that phenomenology as a method cannot suspend the question of ontology. And I agree with him, as I have said elsewhere (Mills, 2010, 2012). But I do not agree that we cannot criticize certain transpersonal or supernatural frameworks,[2] such as onto-theism, because we may use the same criterion to adjudicate their validity based upon onto-phenomenology. The question becomes, Do they empirically manifest or appear? Just as an archetype must appear in order to be actual, so must Spirit (*Geist*) or God. Spirit or soul emerges in all things that are psychic by virtue of the fact that we are alive and the world is animated with life, while God, which I argue is a human concept of ultimate Ideality as the invention of an idea, *does not* for the simple reason that God has not manifested. Point me to the empirical evidence if I am wrong. Furthermore, an "apparent interiority" is not the same as apparent exteriority, as following Goodwyn's logic, each phenomenon should have to justify a material existence. Internality and externality are equiprimordial: they are two dimensions of spacetime yoked together ontically in psyche.

Given that inner and outer are phenomenal experiences within mind transpiring within aspects and magnitudes of worlding, and that division, splitting, bifurcation of otherness, identity, and difference are dialectical relations we categorize in thought itself, I do not follow the criticism that we cannot posit these contrary distinctions internally without falling back on some grand metaphysical scheme. On the contrary, this approach can explain internal dynamics without having to offer, let alone figure out, the big picture item of a formal metaphysics of the cosmos. Here, the description of an internal phenomenon follows an idealist methodology due to the fact that it is posited in mind, but that does not mean it does not transpire within a naturalistic-realist schematic: both domains are operative at once on parallel levels and are mutually implicative due to their dialectical relations.

In order to avoid solipsism, viz. everything is in my mind—there is no outside, we start from our own immediacy of experience that is internally given or naturally bestowed then work our way outwardly to a standpoint of externalization of interiority. That is what an archetype does: it awakens from its primal unity in which it finds itself and externalizes its essence into otherness that it then takes back and reabsorbs into its internal structure on a spiraling developmental stairway toward more richer and hardy shapes of expression. This concentric, coiling, ascending stage progression of an archetype constitutes its dialectical awakening, manifestation, and progression.

Presumably when Goodwyn asks, "within what?," he is not satisfied with a purely experiential approach to archetypal process: he is looking for how the psyche is connected to matter in some manner. And not just any matter, but the ultimate or absolute ground that conditions matter itself. In other words, What is more fundamental? He has already alerted us to his position. Goodwyn assumes a top-down monism where "individual psyches are merely local aspects of a much bigger unified substance," such as the implicate order of wholeness that binds us all in our "interconnectedness." As Goodwyn (2020, personal communication) states: "The whole is prior to the part. And thus the most fundamental object is the entire universe, of which everything else is derivative, on down to molecules." There is much to be unpacked in this statement, as it entails having to account for *original first cause*. Here, we may observe a revival of ancient natural philosophy where he starts macrocosmically with the whole universe and then microcosmically locates the "real" substance in the atom. In my approach, I do not have to provide my own cosmogony to address the questions of how an archetype manifests while Goodwyn does. He presupposes a physical cosmos in which matter, mind, psyche, and *arché* all emerge out of. Having said this, my position does not necessarily contradict his, as essence must not only appear, it must be connected, at least theoretically, to all other forms of entities (actual or potential) in a monistic universe where everything is interconnected and ontically interdependent, or it could not disperse its essence in the first place let alone intermingle or participate of a shared universe. It is only on the condition that we participate of one cosmos that essence can intermingle with all objects (in thought, proximity, spacetime) or else we would have an infinite sea of plurality with incompatible essences due to their different internal structures, processes, and properties that by definition *could not* intermingle. That is why patterns must be universal in some form even if their contents, contexts, qualities, properties, intensities, and so on vary.

While I focus on the internality of an archetype, Goodwyn believes they are also "external" to the individual psyche or mind, presumably due to cross-cultural symbols, and this would likely align him in some way with Jung's notion of the collective unconscious or objective psyche. But, we could claim there are only collective psyches that participate of universal essences even if they derive or come from one source. Regardless, I am starting from "within" and Goodwyn is starting from "without," which is justified within a dual-aspect or neutral monist paragon where everything emanates from and trickles back to "the origin of which is the 'neutral substance'." This is the Neoplatonic pole of his thinking that in many ways attempts to account for first cause, first substance, and the overarching paradigm that, if I am reading him correctly, posits a cosmic emanationist philosophy of transpersonal supervenience reminiscent of panpsychism. Here, psyche (he refers to them as individual egos) emerges from our generic "impersonal substrata" that is the universal a priori condition for mind to materialize. Whether we situate these ideas and aporias in the history of substance philosophy, Ideal Forms, panpsychism, contemporary mind studies, and/or theoretical physics that promise a unified concept of mind and nature, I will leave that for him to resolve. Current trends in Jung studies have been keen to explore the relationship between participation and transpersonal psychology (Brown, 2020) and have even linked the psyche with singularity and holographic string theory where, taken from Jung's (1952) equation relating psychic energy to mass: "Psyche = highest intensity in the smallest space" (p. 45), the ultimate archetype of unity (symbolized by the mandala) unites cosmos and psyche in a singular underlying structure (Desmond, 2018). Whether or not Goodwyn privileges metaphysics over onto-phenomenology, mystical moments of unitive experience may be said to comport well within a monistic ontology.

I think professor Goodwyn has more cut out for himself to prove than I do by simply adopting an onto-phenomenal praxis because its stays experientially-near rather than experientially-far. In other words, remaining within a theoretical model that describes and explicates the process of immediate experiential mediacy and the dialectical unfolding of internal ontology has less burden than accounting for, let alone proving, the existence of a mind independent universe from which all is said to derive from and that *is itself psychic*, not to mention how that is possible. He has already committed to privileging ontological realism that conditions all other forms of substance to derive from and manifest, including the psyche or mind itself, but he also makes psyche derivative of a cosmic panpsychic process that supervenes on all particularities that populate the universe, which I believe is a logical corollary to his proposition. Can we further lend credibility to this thesis?

On holism

All of this engages the question of holism. Goodwyn takes my remarks on the transcendent function and pursuit of wholeness (Mills, 2018, p. 210) as being "either an infantile desire or an imaginary concept" when he is invested, understandably so, in seeing how everything fits within the whole as a unified monism. Recent scholarship in holism and its problematics have addressed this question, along with its limitations, in depth (McMillan, Main, & Henderson, 2020; Main, Henderson, & McMillan, 2020). For the record, I do not see how holism neatly fits within a unified metaphysics despite my training in process philosophy except from the standpoint of abstract theory, logic, or mystical encounters of lived reality. It clearly is not possible from a psychological vantage point as we can never be complete or totally unified in our being, as this would mark the end of desire. Name me one human being who does not lack? The pursuit of wholeness is an infinite striving to fulfill oneself, to achieve ideality, to broach completion, such as the individuation process affords, hence to end the lack; but this is only possible, if at all (if we are lucky, and only as an emotional attitude), when we perish: the striving itself, therefore, is a necessary transcendental illusion that brings qualitative zest to life. This does not devalue the impetus and felt-need for wholeness, only that we must realize the delimitations of such a grandiloquent quest. The most we can hope for is that we gain increasing approximations to this mode of ideal value. The transcendent function as process offers no guarantees that opposition will ever be unified or fully sublated, only engaged, wrestled with, and savored for its own value. Here, we must concede that the phenomenal felt-attitude can be entirely different from its ontological attainment.

Goodwyn wants me to take a stand on my "underlying metaphysical assumptions about the nature of what psyche actually is," that is, "what sort of substance psyche is or not...You have to take a position on what sort of thing psyche *is* first and justify it before you can then subsequently explain why such things are unreal, incoherent, or implausible. Mills only does half the work needed here to make such claims." We can try to bracket this demand through onto-phenomenology, as I have tried to do, but he is ultimately correct: we can never elude metaphysics because it "always has a way of coming back to bite us in the ass" (Mills, 2020b, p. 195). More on this in a moment.

Psyworld

I have attempted to argue that an archetype must externalize itself in nature (including the material-energetic world of mind-brain dependence) in order for it to be made actual (Mills, 2018), but nature (the physical universe) may very well be the original condition from which it derives and emerges, hence making the distinction only important based on first principles, namely, original ground (*ab origine*). An onto-phenomenological scheme allows us to enter the dialectical circle anywhere in the system and still be connected to the whole, but from a particular perspective as ontological relativity within the multiplicities of Being. This methodology has its own problems, which I will not pretend to resolve here. Although the universe is there for consciousness, and we find ourselves in it, of which psyche is a part of, its relation to an endless holism all the way to infinity is not something I can defend in the scope of this project. I look forward to further discussions with professor Goodwyn on this enjoyable topic where we largely share a simpatico in intellectual interest and fellowship, but I would like to end with some preliminary speculations on first principles of which we are both preoccupied with.

Roger Brooke (2015, cf. p. 80) has made the claim, following in both an epistemological and phenomenological tradition via Jung, that "we are in psyche," not that "psyche is in us." As he puts it elsewhere, "the psyche is the world in which we live and find ourselves. It is not inside us; we are inside it" (Brooke, 2009, p. 604). Here, he is amplifying on Jung (1957, p. 271) who says that psyche *surrounds* us, and is not merely in us, as our encounter with life includes all of worldhood. Jung also extends this to the collective unconscious that "surrounds us on all sides," and like psyche is "an atmosphere in which we live" (Jung, 1946, p. 433). Being within, surrounded by, and in an atmosphere spatializes the psyche as an encompassing principle of presence that, like the concept of world, follows a philosophy of containment. Here, the notion of a whole is implicit and presupposed when we postulate an out-side that contains all within. The locus is a shift from the inner to the outer that conditions the inner, but at the same time, is indistinguishable from its point(s) of origin.

Brooke goes to great length to differentiate the psyche from the mind, as he abhors the reductive language of reification and any philosophi-cal implications that separates mind from world, which he sees as a post-renaissance creation. For Brooke (2009), following Husserl and his pupil Martin Heidegger, psyche is the lifeworld (*Lebenswelt*): "The world is thus the place of psychological life ...the landscape of my psychic life" (p. 603). In other words, the world is for me as I am immersed in my thrownness into the (a) symbolic, hence the archetypal, language and narrative, culture, (b) history and cosmos; and (c) into a *psychology of place*, hence my environ-ment, my body, things, objects of perception, which are ready at hand, and so forth mediated through discourse (*logos*) and spatiotemporal relations as our being in the world.

Let us take this up for a moment that Psyche surrounds us, is an atmos-phere in which we are embedded and live, and we are in worldhood rather than it being in us, like our brains. But we can go further than this: *we are psyche*. Let's call this *psyworld*, a symbiosis between embodiment and expe-rience. The psyworld is that which we are, at once given or thrown, in the sense that we must encounter and grasp the situation or facticity in which we find ourselves, *before* any moment of self-reflection or analysis, that is, before an observing conscious ego develops simply because we are *inside* the situation—materially, environmentally, culturally; and every develop-mental experience the self has with the world thereafter that has been incor-porated, modified, memorialized, and laid down mnemonically within the interiors and contours of its unconscious abyss. The reason why psyworld is given is that we are in it already as being-in-experience—its original state or condition, as life that desires within us. This original *that* or *something* that bears itself before us is identical to what presents itself to us as who we are in such immediacy. The moment self-reflexivity occurs, the minute an observ-ing ego-consciousness or self-consciousness is introduced, the ego breaches the immediacy of its naked thereness, its original being—the *thisness* of psy-che, its primal unconscious ontology. When self-reflection ensues, we move from direct emersion in our primordiality to an objectification of the plural-ity of things which we are part of, yet remain and occur within our original being. As such, it is the reality within us.[3] Psyworld is therefore everything we find ourselves in and experience throughout life informed by all pres-ences and intensities it encounters, both in terms of its embodied physical existence, the materiality of the natural world, and the social relations in which it is embedded.

This attitude adopts realism as an ontological prior, which logically precedes the individual subject by virtue of the fact that we are born into a preexisting material and environmental reality. But this does not negate idealistic currents inherent in a naturalized attitude; rather, both processes are co-occurrences operating simultaneously. This position takes a stand on what is primary and what ontological conditions exist prior to our own personal existence. The question of whether psyche comes *before* the human being vis-à-vis the collective unconscious is another matter. Furthermore, the question of whether psyche participates of a universal panpsychism I will suspend: I am not prepared to make that commitment without having investigated the matter in depth. But all these conditions would still assume a naturalized form of existence, perhaps even transpersonal or transcendental (however that is defined) that prefaces each of our psychological lives, which clearly emphasizes a concrete world of objects and processes prior to human consciousness. But psyworld is more than just the material world alone: it is its own bracing and restoring cosmos. When one gets tired of physics, one finds "meta," something beyond or *more than* just the antiseptic universe of physical objects. Here, psyche is *lifesoul* that enlivens its own world, one that surrounds us in its own atmosphere of vitality and containment.

Regardless of what position we take on these matters, these distinctions and qualifications continue to dog metaphysics by vexing questions introduced by the epistemological turn. How do we know the world exists without psyche? How do we know the world is merely what we experience? How do we know anything is whole or contained under a unification principle? What does whole mean? Non-division, non-difference? Difference within totality? Then, how can anything be unified, let alone singular or one? If it is everything, then how do we know a world exists at all when it could merely be psyche that exists and the universe (us included) is its product and manifestation? If the universe is psychic, how could non-organic life have consciousness, especially since the concept of consciousness is a modern invention? How about an executive agency or central control station running the railroad? These questions naturally address Goodwyn's concerns as well. But unlike Goodwyn and Brooke, I am interested in internal spacings, largely derived from or modified by unconscious factors, and this is more of a categorical distinction or feature of interiority belonging to onto-phenomenal processes or internal ontology than it is on the big ticket item of, What comes first, chicken or egg? Regardless of what causal antecedents we may attribute to ultimate genesis, inner and outer, within and without, internal and external are equiprimordial. In other words, they are inseparable and mutually implicative because they are dynamic dialectical relations that cannot exist without the other. We experience these diversities and demarcations phenomenologically within different modes of being and awareness. Just as we have various ontic and existentiell relations to people and place, we also filter and experience them internally through various intuited, perceived, or felt boundaries of distinction, separation, and occasion. To assume no boundaries between inner and outer, undifferentiated unity or holism, complete totality or wholeness, then Oneness is merely a phenomenological or mystical encounter, which is not the same as a metaphysical singularity.

Esse in anima

There are very scant references by Jung to *esse in anima*. He first refers to the term in *Psychological Types*, and his entire discussion takes place in the context of the question of the existence of God. Although customarily translated as "being in the soul," we may wish to highlight the verb "to *be* in soul." For Jung (1921), to be in soul was given: "The *esse in anima*, then, is a psychological fact, and the only thing that needs ascertaining is whether it occurs but once, often, or universally in human psychology" (*CW*, 6, § 67). *Esse in anima* is introduced as a "third, mediating standpoint" (*CW*, 6, § 77) between mind (*nous*) or intellect (*intellectu*) and material reality or things (*re*) united in and through psyche as a fusion of opposite substances (material, immaterial, or otherwise). Here, *esse in anima* has the same meaning as the "human psyche," which Jung employs interchangeably in this early book, only then to abandon its usage altogether. Instead, he adopts the conventional term "psychic reality" that was then later recast under the guise of the psychoid.

Jung, over and over years, emphasizes the "autonomous activity of the psyche" as a "vital process, a continually creative act" (*CW*, 6, § 78). Soul has vitality and creates as it acts. This leads Jung to claim: "The psyche creates reality everyday" (*CW*, 6, § 78). But what does he mean by that? The answer is not surprising but it is important. Here, Jung is not adopting a pure idealism where the soul thinks its existence into being nor the material reality of the external world, but rather reality is created via *"fantasy"* (*CW*, 6, § 78). In other words, fantasy is its own reality. Fantasy becomes the "bridge" between subject and object, where "inner and outer worlds are joined together in living union" (*CW*, 6, § 78) mediated through unconscious process. Here, Jung adopts a particular position that was well embraced by German Idealism: imagination mediates between intuition (perception of objects) and thought (ideas). And for Hegel (1830), "phantasy is reason" (§ 457). *Geist*— meaning both "spirit" and "mind"—and nature (*Natur*) are united: the subject–object divide is closed. For Jung, soul is an aperture that provides a porthole to consciousness *and* heaven through the powers of imagination.

Scholarly engagement of the concept of *esse in anima* is esoteric and largely related to commentary on the autonomy of the psyche following a generative principle (Novac, 2013), as a solution to the problem of the Cartesian split (Colman, 2017), Jung's foundationalist epistemology (Brooks, 2011), on the question of grounding psychic experience (McMillan, 2016), and the realm of the psychoid (Bishop, 2000; Brooks, 2011; Huskinson, 2003; Mills, 2014a). Christian McMillan (2018) has analyzed the inherent vitalism in Jung's notion of soul as "an 'opening' to an enchanted sensation" (p. 195), but further alerts us to the problem of Jung's fluidity and blurring of boundaries. Steve Myers (2019) has emphasized how *esse in anima* co-creates the world we experience as a matrix of interactions between our perceptual apparatus and the external environment mediated through an implicit unconscious epistemology. Robin McCoy Brooks (2011) has further interpreted Jung's concept of *esse in anima* as signifying the notion that "being resides in the soul" (p. 498). For Jung, the psyche provides "its living value" (*CW*, 6, § 77): it confers its own being. "What indeed is reality if it is not a reality in ourselves, an *esse in anima*?" (*CW*, 6, § 77). Here, existence has a surplus of value: psyche is "living being" (Jung, 1926; *CW*, 8, § 605).

What does it mean for being to reside in soul? Would this not make the unconscious the house of Being?[4] What is reality, if it is granted as life within? Is this not tantamount to an unconscious phenomenology or does it signify more? How do these ideas correlate with my notion of psyworld? Keeping in mind the problem of boundaries of the psyche, I wish to exploratorily offer six propositional attitudes from the standpoint of onto-phenomenology:

1: Psyche is existence

Psyche is real, that which *is*, that which is the case. We *are* psyche—living reality: it is our facticity. We fall into psyche and awaken as psyche strikes into existence. Psyworld is there, standing before itself, as offering, as inner being, self-presence.

2: Psyche is experience

Psyche experiences and is experiencing. We are experience: we experience ourselves, experience world, and have experience of experiencing. Psyworld is source point: pure experience, pure process, continuous flow, unrest. Nothing is outside of psychic experience, as outside is an internal posit. All boundaries are psychic boundaries: created, demolished, erased. Psyworld is its own fashioning.

3: Psyche creates world

Psyche exists and world is its product and manifestation. Worldhood is conceived in psyche. Psyche awakens as desire and sentience and knows itself as self-certainty, its intuited and felt interiority, which it superimposes on all events it encounters, both within and outside the boundaries it forges within itself. Because psyworld encounters itself as already being *in* experience, it apprehends the manifold of existence as a creative and fluid act, uniquely filtered through its internal naturalized subjectivity. Psyche is therefore generative and procreative. Reality is constructed and reconstructed by mind.

4: Psyche is not in the world, but rather world is in psyche

Psyche is world. World is already bracketed *in*. Psyworld contains the full plurality of reality. We can never get outside of psyche, only posit divisions, fissures, distinctions, and difference within identity. Objectification is merely a partitioning off and reorganization of what it apprehends as world, one that presents itself to itself as living reality, being-in-soul.

5: The world is psyche

We are born inside world and generate world: psyworld is interiorized and interiorizing. World is presented *to* and is presented *in* psyche as presence. Psyworld is self-presencing. Psyche imbues world with its essence. Psyworld is an expanse of *spacings* and temporal dispersal of interiority. Reality is therefore psychic, the mediation and encircling of world.

6: Psyche is world

We are world; world is us. World is enveloped within psyche. Psyche encompasses and encloses the whole of world and everything it experiences. Psyworld is in itself and from itself, as Being-in-and-for-itself. Psyche is psyworld. Psyworld is its own universe.

Coda

We have determined that *esse in anima* as being *in* psyche is ontologically determined yet determinate as its own psyworld, which may be viewed as a border concept bridging and integrating natural embodiment and the encompassing experiential lifeworld it encounters as a synthetic existential unit. We are a psyworld of our own making yet already endowed as its own existence disclosed as being-in-experience. Psyche encounters world as a totality, first from its most inchoate or nascent condition of simple unity it finds itself ensconced, to the breach into plurality and multiplicities of entities and environs it differentiates itself from, which populate world. Here psyworld breaks out of its indivisible immediate being it finds itself submerged and engrossed as archetypal embryo only then to generate a manifold world of different objects by the spatiotemporal act of splitting up unity into particularization and plurality. Emersion in immediate unity leads to dispersal, which leads to a regathering of its essence conjoined in a much greater totality of inclusion as a culminating wholeness in thought and being. Whether this extends to Being itself remains a mystery.

Just as we have articulated the essence and internal ontology of an archetype, this paradigmatic structural and patterned activity must apply to the psyche itself as a developmental, epigenetic, architectonic monistic process of becoming. In other words, essence must permeate every aspect of psychic reality in order to participate of a greater holistic process. Whether psyche returns to a *higher unity* throughout its developmental maturation toward the pursuit of wholeness requires more study. These preliminary conclusions based on speculative metaphysics may lead to more applications and justifications from other disciplines interested in abductive and empirical demonstration. Whether psyche is the foundation of everything, where the whole is Psyworld, and that everything else is merely a variation and extraction of cosmic Mind, is left unanswered.

Notes

1 See David Henderson (2014) who also explores the conundrum of opposites in his apophatic engagement of Jung.
2 Please note that when I refer to the "transpersonal" I am referring to phenomena that are beyond individualistic experience and expression, such as universals common to social collectives (Mills, 2019a), spirituality or religious instinct being a prime example; but when I refer to "supernatural," I mean a supreme Creator or Being (or entities) that is above or beyond the natural universe in which we find ourselves, not to mention the more pedestrian definitional notions of God enjoyed by the masses, a subject matter I have thoroughly refuted (Mills, 2017).
3 Cf. Jung (1927): "For it is the function of consciousness not only to recognize and assimilate the external world through the gateway of the senses, but to translate into visible reality the world within us" (*CW*, 8 § 342).
4 Although I make this point in *Origins* (Mills, 2010, p. 66), in my analysis of Heidegger's project of fundamental ontology, I make the argument that the unconscious is the house of Being rather than language (Cf. Mills, 2014b, p. 289).

References

Bishop, P. (2000). *Synchronicity and Intellectual Intuition ns Kant, Swedenborg, and Jung*. Lewiston, NY: Edwin Mellen Press.
Brooke, R. (2009). The self, the psyche, and the world: A phenomenological interpretation. *Journal of Analytic Psychology*, 54: 601–618.
Brooke, R. (2015). *Jung and Phenomenology: Classic Edition*. London: Routledge.
Brooks, R.McCoy (2011). Un-thought out metaphysics in analytical psychology: A critique of Jung's epistemological basis for psychic reality. *Journal of Analytical Psychology*, 56: 492–513.
Brown, R.S. (2020). *Groundwork for a Transpersonal Psychoanalysis*. London: Routledge.
Colman, W. (2017). Soul in the world: Symbolic culture as the medium for psyche. *Journal of Analytical Psychology*, 62(1): 32–49.
Desmond, T. (2018). *Psyche and Singularity: Jungian Psychology and Holographic String Theory*. Nashville, TN: Persistent Press.
Goodwyn, E.D. (2010). Approaching archetypes: Reconsidering innateness. *Journal of Analytical Psychology*, 55: 502–521.

Goodwyn, E.D. (2013). Recurrent motifs as resonant attractor states in the narrative field: A testable model of the archetype. *Journal of Analytical Psychology*, 58: 387–408.

Goodwyn, E.D. (2019). Jung and the Mind-Body Problem. In J. Mills (Ed.), *Jung and Philosophy* (pp. 67–85). London: Routledge.

Goodwyn, E.D. (2020a). Archetypal origins: Biology vs culture is a false dichotomy. *International Journal of Jungian Studies*, 13 (2): 111–129.

Goodwyn, E.D. (2020b). Commentary on Mills' "The Essence of Archetypes." *International Journal of Jungian Studies*, 12(2): 207–216.

Hegel, G.W.F. (1830). Philosophy of spirit. In M.J. Petry (Ed.), *Hegel's Philosophy of Subjective Spirit*. Vol. 3: *Phenomenology and Psychology*. (Trans). Dordrecht, Holland: D. Reidel Publishing Company, 1978.

Henderson, D. (2014). *Apophatic Elements in the Theory and Practice of Psychoanalysis*. London: Routledge.

Huskinson, L. (2003). *Nietzsche and Jung*. New York: Brunner-Routledge.

Jung, C.G. (1953–1977). *Collected Works of C.G. Jung*; Bollingen Series, 20 vols. Eds. H. Read, M. Fordham, G. Adler; Trans. R.F.C. Hull. London: Routledge & Kegan Paul; Princeton: Princeton University Press. (Hereafter referred to *CW* by vol. no.)

Jung, C.G. (1921). *Psychological Types. CW*, 6.

Jung, C.G. (1926). Spirit and Life. *CW*, 8: 319–337.

Jung, C.G. (1927). The Structure of the Psyche. *CW*, 8: 139–158.

Jung, C.G. (1946/1973). Letter to Fritz Künkel 10 July. *Letters of C.G. Jung. Vol. I: 1906-1950*. Princeton, NJ: Princeton University Press.

Jung, C.G. (1952/1973). Leap Year Letter to John Raymond Smythies, 29 February. *Letters of C.G. Jung. Vol. II: 1951-1961*. Princeton, NJ: Princeton University Press.

Jung, C.G. (1952). Answer to Job. *CW*, 11: 355–470.

Jung, C.G. (1957). The Undiscovered Self. *CW*, 10: 245–305.

Main, R., Henderson, D., and McMillan, C. (Eds.) (2020). *Jung, Deleuze, and the Problematic Whole*. London: Routledge.

McMillan, C. (2016). *Esse in Anima*: The problem of grounding between jung and deleuze. https://oneworldprojectholism.files.wordpress.com/2016/07/esse-in-anima-the-problem-of-grounding-between-jung-and-deleuze.pdf. Downloaded May 25, 2020.

McMillan, C.(2018). Jung and Deleuze: Enchanted openings to the other: A philosophical contribution. *International Journal of Jungian Studies*, 10(3): 184–198.

McMillan, C., Main, R., and Henderson, D. (Eds.) (2020). *Holism: Possibilities and Problems*. London: Routledge.

Mills, J. (2002). Five Dangers of Materialism. *Genetic, Social, and General Psychology Monographs*, 128(1): 5–27. Reprinted in Marion, M. (2004) (Ed.), *Taking Sides: Clashing Views on Controversial Issues in Cognitive Science* (pp. 10–19). Dubuque, IA: McGraw-Hill/Dushkin.

Mills, J. (2010). *Origins: On the Genesis of Psychic Reality*. Montreal: McGill-Queens University Press.

Mills, J. (2012). *Conundrums: A Critique of Contemporary Psychoanalysis*. New York: Routledge.

Mills, J. (2014a). Jung as philosopher: Archetypes, the psychoid factor, and the question of the supernatural. *International Journal of Jungian Studies*, 6 (3): 227–242.

Mills, J. (2014b). Truth. *Journal of the American Psychoanalytic Association*, 62(2): 267–293. doi:10.1177/0003065114529458

Mills, J. (2017). *Inventing God: Psychology of Belief and the Rise of Secular Spirituality*. London: Routledge.

Mills, J. (2018). The essence of archetypes. *International Journal of Jungian Studies*, 10 (3): 199–220.

Mills, J. (2019a). The myth of the collective unconscious. *Journal of the History of the Behavioral Sciences*, 55: 40–53.

Mills, J. (2019b). Psyche as inner contradiction. *Continental Thought & Theory: A Journal of Intellectual Freedom*, 2(4): 71–82.

Mills, J. (2020a). On the origins of archetypes. *International Journal of Jungian Studies*, 12(2): 201–206.

Mills, J. (2020b). The essence of myth. *Journal of Indian Council of Philosophical Research*, 37(2): 191–205. doi:10.1007/s40961-020-00198-3.

Myers, S. (2019). *Myers-Briggs Typology vs Jungian Individuation*. London: Routledge.

Novac, I.-M. (2013). *Esse in Anima*: C.G. Jung's phenomenological ontology. In M. Marsonet and G. Rață (Eds.), *Applied Social Science: Science and Theology* (pp. 79–87). Newcastle, UK: Cambridge Scholars.

Chapter 6

The origins of psyche

From experience to ontology

Erik Goodwyn

Introduction

In his latest essay, Mills (2020, see also Mills, 2018) covers many of my initial concerns adequately but raises new challenges for me to engage with. Crucially, he points out that the metaphysical framework I use to understand archetypes begins from "without"—i.e., that I assume a foundational neutral substance that emanates both psyche and matter that is "reminiscent of panpsychism".

We will get to panpsychism later, but for now, Mills is correct when he states:

> Goodwyn has more cut out for himself to prove than I do by simply adopting an onto-phenomenal praxis because it stays experientially-near rather than experientially-far. In other words, remaining within a theoretical model that describes and explicates the process of immediate experiential mediacy and the dialectical unfolding of internal ontology has less burden than accounting for, let alone proving, the existence of a mind independent universe from which all is said to derive from and that *is itself psychic,* not to mention how that is possible. He has already committed to privileging ontological realism that conditions all other forms of substance to derive from and manifest, including the psyche or mind itself, but he also makes psyche derivative of a cosmic panpsychic process that supervenes on all particularities that populate the universe, which I believe is a logical corollary to his proposition.

From primary experience to beyond

I will attempt to rise to Professor Mills' challenge by seeing if there is a way to start from the experientially-near that can lead, logically, to the experientially-far. I begin with a single postulate.

DOI: 10.4324/9781003349921-6

Postulate 1: Phenomenal experience (mind) exists

This may be the most indisputable element of this whole discussion and is defended very nicely by Goff (2017). That phenomenal experience *in itself* exists, there can be no reasonable dispute (though see Dennett, 1988 and counter-argument in Goodwyn, 2021a). Sure, the entire universe I see may be a hallucination, but I cannot deny that *I am hallucinating something*. In any case, this event is what we mean when we say "mind", "experience" or "consciousness"—I will use these and "psyche" interchangeably. In any case, whatever phenomenal experience is, it has certain characteristics that we must remain cognizant of: that is, this phenomenal experience typically is of *coherent and unified* phenomena, often accompanied by a concomitant phenomenal impression of "separateness" between the experiencer and that which is experienced (hallucinatory or not). Note the scare quotes are essential, in order to remain free of metaphysical assertion prematurely, as this *impression* of separateness may or may not reflect true metaphysical distinction. This postulate is quite a bit more powerful than it might first appear, as we will see later.

For now, within this mind, we arrive quickly at three conceptual divisions of psychic contents: ego ("my mind"), apparently-minded-but-not-ego ("other minds"), and apparently-non-minded-non-ego ("matter"). More on these in a moment. For now, I want to state clearly what my main questions are about this foundational starting point:

1   From what (if anything) does the grounding for these entities derive?
2   How do they relate to one another?
3   Are any of these *metaphysically* separate, rather than only *conceptually/experientially* separate?

Let's try to set up a way to answer question #1. Where does all of this come from? Mills seems to be content with the "the psyche itself", which is a logical answer, but it is vulnerable to the accusation of being a tautology. After all, if we define psyche to be subjectively experienced events in all their sensory and vivid glory, saying that such things come from "the psyche" is saying that the experiences come from themselves.

And yet, there is reason to believe this is not a tautology. To say that the psyche *exists* is to say that it has ontological status—i.e., it is fully real. Not only does this postulate feel quite reasonable—after all, if it does not exist, what is it? (Some say "an illusion", but this explanation is contradictory, see Goodwyn, 2021a)—it tells us that psyche itself has ontological status. This is *not* to say that the *contents* and *subject matter* of psyche is always real. Square circles and other contradictory or incoherent concepts, for example, cannot be real. But that is not what the postulate is saying. It is saying that *psyche itself is real*. Hence I am real, because "I" appears to be inseparable from psyche—there is always a subject because psyche consists of experience. Since experience happening to nothing is contradictory, some kind of ego must exist when psyche exists. This property of psyche is classically defended as its intrinsic intentionality or "aboutness" (Brentano, 1874).

Thus, we arrive at the conclusion that psyche exists, is fully real, and it depicts various categories as its contents, one of which comes to be labeled "myself"—i.e the *subject* of psychic contents, which is also real, even if the other contents are not necessarily real. I use scare quotes here because we will have to bracket the question of exactly what a "self" strictly is since that would take us far afield. Rather, let's define the self loosely, in the manner of Jung, as merely the conscious egoic part of the human psyche in which I subjectively find myself—indeed it *is* the "I". Beyond this part exists the other categories of experience that include experiences deemed as non-ego (i.e, other minded selves and non-minded entities and everything in between). On this, I believe Mills and I would agree.

Now, we are prepared to tackle question 1: where does psyche itself *come from*? We appear to have two possibilities to avoid infinite regression: identify that psyche is itself ultimately unanalyzable and brute, or that it derives from something else. Again, this is not as simple as it first appears. It does seem to my reading, however, that Mills wishes to, in the manner of phenomenology, bracket this question and focus his attention on the characteristics and behavior psyche displays, rather than trouble ourselves with its origin. We are, after all, thrown into it *in medias res* without explanation and we need to deal with it. On the other hand, as he often speaks of psyche as being ground that itself needs no grounding, one might interpret that to mean he feels the former answer is best—i.e., that psyche is unanalyzable and brute. If so, however, it does not quite halt the enterprise, because even if we assume psyche is brute, as it may very well be, we can still ask ourselves how psyche itself *relates* to the other categories of experience, or indeed even *if* it relates.

As mentioned, it appears that Mills chooses to bracket the question for the time being, even though he gives good reason to suppose psyche is brute. Bracketing is, of course, an acceptable strategy, provided we recognize that it limits our ability to make certain determinations. Thus, it is also my opinion that pursuing what the origin of psyche is, and hence venturing into the risky territory beyond the brackets can lead us to some conclusions about psychic behavior that we might not otherwise see, and ultimately may shed more light on what archetypes are. What Mills has inspired me to do is to be more careful about this enterprise and venture beyond the boundaries and see if we can get to the "experientially far" from *his* starting point.

Of bioscience and brackets

My goal for this essay, therefore, is to see if there is a way to push the boundaries of the brackets toward the question of where the psyche comes from beyond the immediately phenomenological starting point Mills uses, but keeping in the spirit of a phenomenological approach that warns strongly against unjustified reduction or epistemological presuppositions. From there, we can continue the discussion about archetypes from common ground. But let's stop here, then, to reiterate our first conclusion:

Conclusion 1: Psyche exists, and I (currently) exist within it.

If there was no "I", of course, there would be no one to ask the question of whether or not it exists, thus it would be incoherent to say it doesn't. For now, since we have established that psyche is real, we can fairly ask how it originates. But to answer that question, we risk making just such an error of presupposition if we try to account for *all* of psyche before we at least try to account for our *own* (i.e., the local, my-ego-affiliated piece of) psyche, though we have not determined whether or not psyche continuously exists everywhere or is localized somehow temporospatially. We are, after all, trying to stay experientially near. So, let us start more humbly with: given that *I* exist, can I use that knowledge to learn about the reality of anything else that I experience?

What strikes us beyond "I exist" is that there appear to be *other* minds out there that feel subjectively similar to ours. That is, in the field of experience, there appear to be other entities who behave *as if* they were having experiences like ours, even if we can't feel those experiences ourselves. Conclusion 1, of course, does not state that I am the *only* ego to exist. Thus, it seems fair to suppose that others do, too. But, can I prove it? The existence of other minds is a classic problem, since there appears to be no evidence to suggest those other entities are actually *minds* with ontological status as mine is, rather than a solipsistic illusion. This lack of evidence, however, must square with the perhaps equally vexing issue that we have no direct evidence *against* it. We cannot say that either state has default preference which requires that the burden of proof rest with the other alternative. In phenomenology, that would be a mistake because the very existence of experiences-deemed-other-minds already presents itself to consciousness and must therefore be accounted for somehow, and you could just as easily argue that the burden of proof rests with the claimant to somehow prove that it is *not* exactly what it appears to be—in this case, another mind with experiences similar to ours. Postulating possible Cartesian demons who wish to deceive us, or outlandish brain-in-vat scenarios seems *more* preposterous, not less, than simply tentatively accepting that such experiences are what they appear to be until proven otherwise. The parsimonious alternative, then, is that other minds exist and are fully real.

It's not proof, but it's a start. There is, however, one possible fact that may tip the scale in favor of pro-other experiential reality: the fact that we *feel so strongly* that it is so, even without rational justification. Could this be an illusion? Sure, and yet, the consequences of this belief or non-belief seem monumental: if I dismiss the feeling that others feel as I do, I can justify acts toward them that would otherwise be deemed morally repugnant, which itself evokes disgust and aversion, both of which strike the ego just as strongly as if by sticks or stones. If I accept it as true, however, I find myself in line with these other independent impressions. This is perhaps not "proof" either, but then again, it is only fair of us to ask at this point: what sort of proof might be forthcoming to help us assess the matter beyond a purely feeling-based one as above? I think the phenomenological method forwarded by Mills actually *requires* that we take such feeling-based impressions into account as fully valid evidence, especially considering any other sort of "proof" will be subject to similar doubts. Let us, then, not entertain such doubts unless proven otherwise, and therefore conclude that other minds exist and are similar in some as-yet fully characterized way to ours. This reasoning will help us formulate Conclusion 2:

Conclusion 2: Other minds similar to ours exist

Despite this conclusion, it cannot escape our notice that just as some entities appear to bear the property of mindedness, other entities appear *not* to possess this property. This realization leads us to our final category of psyche: unminded non-ego experiences, i.e., matter. Is "matter" real, and if so, how can we justify it from the onto-phenomenological perspective? I think the everyday experience of change and death is illustrative, provided we meaningfully engage with the *holism* that Mills speaks of in his work. Everyday experience and bioscience reports that entities which present as having the quality of mindedness consistently change when *parts* of them are removed and/or the entity is disintegrated into scattered and isolated components. In other words, collections of objects arranged into integrated wholes which have the property of consciousness individually lose this property when they are separated into heaps of non-interacting parts. Thus far, no one has observed conscious behavior after a person is decapitated or otherwise fatally damaged in some way. Put another way, a severed arm does not itself appear to possess psyche, but the exact same arm *attached to an intact living body* possesses the property of being-a-part-of-a-whole-that-possesses-psyche. This is not to say that the psyche is or is not "in" the arm or anywhere else necessarily (we will get to that later). Rather, I am saying that objects when operating just so together appear to possess psyche can be partitioned into collections of objects that do not.

From this observation, it seems we have the curious phenomenon that psyche is only possessed by densely interacting collections of separable parts—a living brain and body composed of biomolecules working smoothly together—rather than those exact same parts disconnected from each other—i.e dead. The individual parts of experience which are not arranged in just such a manner, therefore, qualify for the category of un-minded non-ego experiences generally aligning with the concept of "matter". That said, because other minds exist (conclusion 2), but strongly correlate with arrangements of parts that appear to be unminded when they are disconnected from one another, it is logical to say that the disintegrated parts which previously formed a minded whole must also exist, since mind being a property of collections of entities that don't exist is contradictory. The extant mind that was possessed by those parts can be said to be an ontologically real *property* of those so-arranged parts, and this property disappears (at least locally—more on that later) when the parts are disconnected from one another. These un-minded parts satisfy our definition of "matter", and thus we can conclude:

> *Conclusion 3: Non-locally-minded matter exists, and can be arranged in just such a way that it gains the local property of mind, and then it can be disintegrated back into isolated parts that themselves do not seem to locally possess mind.*

As we can see, under an onto-phenomenological approach, "matter" is not a given—we have to work to get to it. That's as it should be. In any case, we can combine Conclusions 2 and 3, along with everyday experiences which teach us that there are lawful relations between our bodies and minds. That is, I note that when my toe is stung by a bee, I experience pain, for example, and, of course, life experience along with decades of bioscience reveal many correlations between body behavior and mental experiences in both others and myself. This observation leads us logically to:

> *Conclusion 4: My own mind is a property that is possessed by the matter of which I am composed in a way similar to that of other minds and bodies. Those bits of matter do not appear to possess local mindedness when isolated, but they nonetheless contribute to global mindedness when they are part of a certain kind of whole.*

Now, have it that all three categories of psyche have ontological status—spatiotemporally bounded "matter", and mind, which is a property of properly arranged collections of those otherwise un-minded (or "less" minded) parts. We have gone from my own mind (ego), to other minds, which I infer from the behavior of the bodies associated with those minds, to collections of parts that do not appear to have mind once the parts are disintegrated. I should point out here that these three conclusions do not necessarily equate with a worldview that is identical to the scientific realism Mills attributes to me. For example, if I *dream* of people and mindless objects, those entities qualify as having ontological status under our current analysis. Such objects and people simply have an additional property of apparently only showing up in one temporally bounded episode of my own experience and not others (ignoring parapsychological phenomena). As such, I am not necessarily contradicting Mills' formulation of a "psyworld" when I claim matter, ego, and other persons exist—rather, I believe this refines the definitions within the psyworld. The supposed scientific realist, however, might object to such a claim, arguing that dream characters and objects are not "real", but I think Mills and I both would argue that such a counter-argument has not been justified. Such objects and characters must be accepted as real, but perhaps a different "flavor" of real. I feel I have not strayed from the epistemological boundaries Mills sets up in his proposal of a psyworld, which is only to say we should avoid postulating mind-independent realities since we have no way of knowing if such planes of existence are real, and even dividing entities into things "in themselves" and things "as observed by minds" already presupposes that such a division is itself valid, a Kantian tangle I am not defending here at all.

To summarize:

1 Psyche exists.
2 Because an integral part of psyche is its inclusion of a subject, I exist.
3 Entities present themselves to my own psyche and impress upon me that they possess psyche that is similar to my own.
4 This fact along with moral considerations impel me to propose that those psyches exist as I do.
5 Other entities present themselves as *not* possessing psyche similar to my own—we will call these "matter".
6 Some matter can be arranged just so in a regular and predictable manner that results in the composite objects appearing to possess psyche similar to my own (conception, birth, and growth). By the same token, those composites can be disintegrated, and that results in said psyche disappearing ("death"), while the matter remains.
7 Similarly, parts of my own body that alone do not appear to possess psyche nevertheless *contribute* in a regular and predictable manner to my own psychic *contents*.
8 Since I exist, and changes in matter I attribute to me correlates predictably with changes in my phenomenal experience, and moreover other minds exist and matter correlates with those minds similarly, matter must also exist.

We have thus shown that I, others, and matter exist, but we do not yet know if these three entities are metaphysically separate rather than only conceptually separate. We *can* however, show how these three categories relate to one another beyond what we have already determined.

Bioscience and other everyday things

Bioscience has given us enough evidence to consider that there is some kind of lawful relationship between ego-experience ("mind") and un-minded-non-ego-experience ("matter"). As bioscience progresses, for example, it has become possible to predict, with increasing precision and accuracy, that when a person's brain is behaving in manner X, they will report subjectively experiencing Y. This has, of course, led many to feel strongly that the answer to our first question (where does psyche come from?) must be that psyche is somehow *created by* matter, since in the above data the brain seems to be *causing* the subjective mental event to occur. Thus, in this instance, one might answer the above questions by saying that not only are mind and matter metaphysically separate—which requires us to make the division I just complained about above—but that matter *causes* psyche to emerge. In other words, metaphysicians can propose that the universe is largely mind-independent matter, from which psyche springs up every now and then. Despite my complaints, however, we can at least *justify* the division of the universe into mind-independent reality and minds observing it, *if* the evidence we have gathered from everyday experience and bioscience suggests that it must be true.

The problem here is that bioscience is not actually equipped to make that justification. The data it embodies consists of *correlations*, and correlation is not causation, even if it does suggest that matter and minds are *distinct and connected* in some way yet to be fully characterized. Bioscience does not equip us to assert that matter is more than *conceptually* distinct, and this will not improve with more bioscience, since all it can produce are more and better correlations. This data, therefore, only confirms that matter is a category of psyche that exists in some kind of lawful relation to the category of experience labeled minds (self or other). To demonstrate metaphysical distinction, however, we would need to be able to explain *how* matter creates mind, and bioscience has thus far been woefully unable to even make a wild guess at that, and there are good reasons to think that it is *conceptually incoherent* to attempt it (a fact which itself suggests metaphysical *inseparability*), which I will get to later. In any case, bioscience *does* show us, however, that the behavior of some of the *parts* of those minded entities seems to correlate with such reports in similar ways to how the behavior of our own parts correlates with our own subjectivity. Let's refine Conclusion 4, then:

Conclusion 4 (refined): Other minds report similar experiences that correlate with the behavior of the parts of those entities in a repeatable way to our own correlations between subjective experience and body part behavior. In all cases the behavior of the parts **when isolated** *from the whole is very different from when it is embedded in a whole (i.e. 100 billion neurons arranged into a brain individually behave very differently when they are isolated from one another).*

At this point, then, we have ventured from the experientially-near formulation of psyche, out into the wider realm of what is classically termed the Mind-Body Problem (MBP), that is, how does matter *causally* relate to mind, if at all?

The mind–body problem

I have explored this issue at length (Goodwyn, 2021a,b), but will briefly summarize here, modifying the discussion to keep in line with the onto-phenomenological approach. The most popular attempts to answer the MBP relevant to the current discussion are *physicalism* and *panpsychism*. Both of these approaches venture beyond the brackets by making metaphysical claims about the categories of psyche we have discussed up to this point. Remember, though, that this is fine so long as we have phenomenological justification for it. Let's see if they do.

Physicalism states that *only matter* is fully real and provides the grounding for psyche, which is derivative of matter. Under physicalism, our categories of experience parse out into

1   Matter, which physicalism privileges as having ontological priority.
2   Minds (i.e, psyche), both other and my own, which physicalism asserts are derivative of matter and therefore only secondarily real by virtue of their being created by matter.

Therefore, the physicalist answers question 1 (what is the origin of psyche?) by claiming that matter creates it. Conclusion 1 (I exist) is true insofar as I am reducible to matter, and matter exists. This matter then *creates* the psychic experience I have, and so psyche in itself has a posterior ontological status to matter and is not metaphysically foundational. This psyche then becomes capable of observing, and one of the things it observes (after the fact) is matter, which is how we know about it.

Does this answer to the MBP stretch too far beyond the brackets? On the surface, no, since for all we know psyche *could* be derivative of matter, even though we never experience matter outside of psyche—that could just be an accidental feature of the universe, and the only reason we don't observe it outside of psyche is because "observing" requires psyche to occur. In any case, the justification for physicalism is typically the observation that bioscience continues to show lawful and predictable correlations between matter and psyche, therefore it is presumed that the correlations are due to a causal connection.

The problem with physicalism is that though it asserts that psyche is derivative of matter, it has not thus far been able to provide the derivation. I review the relevant objections to physicalism that have arisen over the years in Goodwyn (2021a), but since Mills is not a physicalist, nor am I, a full review is unnecessary. Briefly: the fact that physicalists cannot satisfyingly account for how matter creates psyche—which remember we have already shown must be real—is not merely a problem of not having enough bioscience at our disposal. The problem is that bioscience only gives us correlations and descriptions without any *explanations*. We can characterize that pain feels the way it does when pain fibers fire in such a way in our bodies, but all additional neuroscience can provide is more and better characterization of the when and the where, but never the *how* or the *why* (causally speaking, that is). They do not at any point address *why* pain fibers behaving in that manner hurts rather than feels like something else entirely different. Since piling on more correlations doesn't get us any closer to that question, it seems extremely likely that we are facing a conceptual incoherence problem rather than a lack-of-data problem. In this case, since the physicalist claims matter creates psyche, it is up to her or him to *justify* how it could do such a thing, and "someday neuroscience will figure it out" is simply not sufficient for a serious analysis.

Panpsychism

While many philosophers continue to holdout that neuroscience will rescue us from this regrettable state, some have decided to abandon the physicalist project and resort to some form or another of *panpsychism*. Panpsychism postulates that psyche cannot be caused by matter because psyche already exists everywhere to one degree or another—i.e., it is brute, in the same way that other properties of the universe (which physicalists do not object to) are brute, such as the speed of light, the Planck constant, or the charge on an electron, or any other properties possessed by whatever physical ultimates physicists discover.

Well and good, as this eliminates the problem created by the physicalist claim. Because psyche (or proto-psyche) already exists everywhere to one degree or another, there is no need to give any explanation for how matter creates it. It is simply a property that exists in the universe that is possessed by some or all of said universe. But this move doesn't quite get us out of trouble: everyday experience reveals that mind appears to be possessed by some collections of matter but not others. Some bodies gain it or lose it, and bioscience can predict very accurately when and under what circumstances. If we reject the physicalist proposal that matter *creates* mind, then why does this regularity of correlation continue to obtain? Can this lawful relation not be explained? Or must the relation between mind and matter necessarily *also* be accepted as brute? That is, do we have any way to explain the *emergence* of more or less of the property of mind in matter-arranged-just-so that does not require matter to "create" it, since that seems unattainable in principle?

Before we look at how panpsychism attempts to answer these questions, we must first distinguish its two broad types: *micropsychism* and *cosmopsychism.* These two types of panpsychism differ on exactly *how* they propose that universe possesses psyche, and they can be differentiated in terms of how they purport to explain human consciousness. We will explore cosmopsychism later, but for now, micropsychism posits that matter possesses psyche at the microscopic level, meaning everything down to physical ultimates like electrons possess psyche, no matter how rudimentary. Under this framework, the human psyche (our anchor point since we know with absolute certainty that it exists) must somehow be the result of the conglomeration of all the micro-psyches coming together to form one macro-psyche.

But, there is a problem here. The very issue physicalists have in explaining how matter creates psyche resurfaces for micropsychism in the so-called combination problem: *why* does jamming together a bunch of micro-psyches create a macro-psyche? As it turns out, this problem has been observed by philosophers to be just as vexing as the physicalist problem (Chalmers, 2016). As I argue in more detail elsewhere, however, *cosmopsychism*, or the framework that proposes that the entire universe possesses consciousness, has neither of these problems, and it also requires the least amount of brute facts to explain all that we have observed up to this point.

A brief summary of this argument (see Goodwyn, 2021a for full details) is as follows: the main issue with both the physicalist problem and the combination problem of micropsychism is that it is a problem of wholes and parts (an early version of this argument can be found in the work of 15th century philosopher Marsilio Ficino, 2001). In keeping with the holism of Mills' psyworld proposal, we must maintain a position that rejects unjustified reduction, and upholds that wholes are more than merely the sum of their parts unless proven otherwise, since this fact is self-evident in everyday consciousness. In other words, properties of wholes cannot always be accounted for by the properties of their isolated parts without strong justification. This strongly holds within the onto-phenomenological approach of Mills and the categories of experience we have discussed thus far. An example from everyday experience is illustrative. The experience of Beethoven's *Ode to Joy* can be broken down into the succession of individual notes that constitute it, but that does not mean the full, unified experience of hearing the melody can be found, even in some fragmentary form, in the isolated note of Middle C (to say nothing of the difference between playing the melody with a full orchestra as opposed to a plastic kazoo). The holistic properties of the experience derive not so much from the notes themselves, but in their *particular arrangement.* Thus, what we are really talking about here are *formal* causes. Put another way, the full experientiality of a collection of sensory impressions has some properties that are not possessed by the individual impressions but only by the *form* all of them take *together.*

Viewed through the lens of this simple fact of onto-phenomenology, and indeed in a holistic mereology in general (Schaffer, 2010), we can immediately see the problem with physicalism and micro-psychism: whether the parts are isolated bits of matter or isolated bits of micro-(proto)-psyche, we are trying to conjure up the property of mindedness in a coherent whole from the properties of the isolated bits. This means the psyche of the whole, which we know exists firsthand, must somehow appear *ex nihilo* when bits are jammed together, because there is no other way to account for it.

Cosmopsychism

These facts of holism and the arrangement of minded objects lead to the conclusion that the micropsychist and physicalist approach may be stymied because they are trying to generate properties of the whole from the properties of isolated parts. This situation is called *pluralism*, and it is the opposite of holism. Holism, rather, states that the relation flows the other way: the properties of parts derive from the wholes from which they were derived. Again, note that such properties of the whole here must imply formal causation—i.e., the properties derive from the form, in which the parts are arranged, not the parts themselves. Put another way, a statue of Zeus is a statue of Zeus regardless of whether it is made of bronze or marble—the form gives it this property, not the material or the efficient causes that led to its creation. Neither marble nor bronze contain proto-Zeus-ness. Therefore, it must be the case that the properties of parts derive from the wholes from which they originated, or (more accurately) from the *form* of the whole in which they participate.

Experience and bioscience has revealed that psyche only appears to be a property of specific *arrangements* of matter—particular organizations of biomolecules that do not appear to have much psyche in themselves when viewed in isolation. This is actually a good (and frequently employed) argument *against* micropsychism. Rocks, for example, do not behave as though they are minded, though, of course, they still *could* be in some mysterious way. But another alternative is that internal rock structure does not have the proper form for this to occur to a significant enough degree.

So, what is the form that correlates with local mindedness, empirically? In general, after decades of bioscience examining brains and bodies, it appears that the condition that correlates with psyche best is the property of *integratedness*. Loosely speaking, integratedness is where each part of a system is highly sensitive to every other part of the system. This property is found in the central nervous systems (CNS) of organisms deemed conscious. Indeed, even *within* the CNS of a human, fluctuations in the parts that are most integrated, such as the frontal lobes, correlate with fluctuations in consciousness whereas fluctuations in areas that are relatively less integrated, like the cerebellum, do *not* correlate with fluctuations in consciousness. Integratedness is, by definition, impossible to achieve in isolated parts and so encourages us to adopt a position of holism with respect to psyche, simply as a result of the data collected by bioscience, even outside of our commitment to it based on the onto-phenomenological approach. Interestingly enough, though, this means *any* system that possesses the requisite amount of integratedness should theoretically possess the property of being minded and have experiences—more on this later.

Emergence and brute facts

Integratedness requires us to employ brute emergence to account for the appearance of psyche in a macroscopic organism in both micropsychism and physicalism. Put another way, it may be the case that macropsyches appearing when bits are arranged just so (whether it is highly integrated or some other yet to be determined form) is itself unanalyzable. Since sooner or later, brute facts are unavoidable, this is acceptable—but surely we can do better than *this*. Within our phenomenological framework, we must acknowledge that we can only speculate as to which metaphysical situation might best account for the existence of psyche. Nevertheless, the impression is unavoidable that the system which has the least amount of brute facts to account for *seems* best, if for no other reason than aesthetics. But aesthetics is in itself a datum that should also be accounted for. We are not, after all, seeking Ultimate Truth (as that would violate our onto-phenomenological approach), but rather the most experientially-near system that we can devise that agrees with all of our experiential data *up to this point* and this must include aesthetic choices.

Thus, when comparing different metaphysical systems, we should consider the one with the fewest brute facts to be the "best", particularly if it has predictive power. Let us see how cosmopsychism fares. Like micropsychism, cosmopsychism proposes that psyche already exists and is brute rather than is derived from matter. Unlike micropsychism, however, cosmopsychism proposes not that human minds exist because they are made up of billions of tiny cellular minds (a pluralist assumption), but rather that human minds exist because they are part of the one *cosmic* consciousness that the universe itself possesses brutely. Cosmopsychism therefore does not require that psyche simply emerge brutely from integrated systems *ex nihilo*, because cosmopsychism is a holistic system—i.e., properties of wholes do not derive from the properties of their parts, but rather the forms that they obtain. For human beings, this means human consciousness will never be found in the properties of isolated neurons—though it is possible for "neuron consciousness" to exist provided neurons are sufficiently integrated themselves. But this is not the same proposal as micropsychism because it is not assumed that human consciousness is *derivative* of neuron consciousness. Rather, neuron consciousness exists because it approaches the *form* needed for consciousness—integratedness, the ultimate example of which is the universe itself. This means that the greatest degree of consciousness—meaning its maximal depth and expansiveness—is likely to correlate with the form of the maximally integrated whole possible, past or present, since forms are atemporal.

Bioscience teaches us that the depth and quality of human consciousness correlates strongly with its integratedness. This is the experientially near anchor point from which we can deduce beyond human consciousness using the regularities revealed by everyday experience as well as bioscience findings. If human consciousness correlates with brain activity, then the property of human consciousness is obtained when the integratedness of the human body (especially the brain) is sufficient. Split brain experiments, traumatic dissociation and other anomalies show us that when integratedness is disrupted, the human body behaves as if it possessed multiple fragmentary consciousnesses. Psychotherapy and other maneuvers seek to *integrate* (in Jungian terms, *individuate*) the human psyche and so foster an expansion of consciousness by increasing integratedness. When this occurs, the previously independent fragmentary conciousnesses (in Jungian terms, *complexes*) work together to contribute to the gradually more holistic and integrated subsequent consciousness.

But this means that systems that are *more* integrated than the human body/brain, but that which we are ourselves nevertheless a part should *also* be conscious, and perhaps even *more so,* though we would have no more immediate awareness of it than the fragmentary consciousness of (say) a single neuron would have of the human being as whole does—barring, of course, parapsychological reports of visions, near-death experiences, altered states, etc. Everyday consciousness operates at the level of local integratedness that it does, with smaller sub-conscious systems operating at their level, but this means trans-human systems sufficiently integrated would also have their own mysterious sort of consciousness. This would apply to systems of humans, or ecosystems, planets, solar-systems, galaxies, on up to the entire universe—provided these systems are sufficiently integrated. Each sub system, furthermore, under holism, would be properly said to *derive* its psyche from the larger system of which it is a part.

Conclusion

Of the main options forwarded thus far—physicalism, micropsychism, and cosmopsychism (and other systems such as idealism and dualism which I have not touched on in this essay)—each has various conceptual issues and challenges, even when informed by the growing body of bioscience. Of these, each requires a set of brute facts to account for:

1   Physicalism proposes that matter exists brutely, and that psyche is created by it in a manner which is also brute. All minds brutely emerge from particular arrangements of matter under physicalism.

2   Micropsychism proposes that psyche exists brutely in every physical ultimate of the universe, and furthermore, when these bits are arranged just
so, human consciousness brutely emerges from such a conglomeration.
3   Unlike the previous two systems, cosmopsychism proposes only that
the universe, as maximally integrated system, has the brutely associated
property of consciousness, and all other consciousnesses are derivative
of that form as part is derivative from whole.
4   Conclusion: cosmopsychism accounts for the origin of psyche and the
relations of the categories within psyche (i.e., matter and minds) in a
way that utilizes the minimum number of brute facts, and it does not entail the combination problem or the corresponding physicalist problem.

One may note, however, that we do not necessarily have to identify the *cosmos* as the origin for consciousness—only the form which brutely associates
with maximum integratedness. The universe, for example, could still merely
be a "heap" of integrated minds that itself does not obtain much integration
between the minds, and so theoretically the universe might not itself be very
conscious. But note that this possibility doesn't really harm the position
of *holistic panpsychism*, since we are saying psyche is brutely a property of
the maximally-integratedness *form*, whatever it may be. This example only
forces us to reject cosmopsychism if the maximally integrated form is not
the cosmos itself. Even in this case, any human consciousness is *still* conscious because it is a however imperfect example of this form, whether or not
the perfect form obtains anywhere in particular.

Does the universe actually represent such a system of maximum integratedness, though? I think we can argue in the affirmative for a few independent reasons (elaborated in more detail in Goodwyn, 2021a). Briefly and first,
the universe is obviously the most inclusive system that exists, and so any
highly integrated system like the human brain will only ever be a part of
the larger universe. This means the universe is potentially more integrated
than a human is, as is any super-system that contains humans in it, such as
populations, ecosystems, galaxies, etc., even if it is only in the same manner
that a human is a little more integrated if it is a brain with a body with all
four limbs rather than three. The difference is small, but it *is* still more integrated. Moreover, there is independent evidence that the universe may be
one giant system that is entangled at the quantum level (Goodwyn, 2021a,
p. 12), meaning every physical ultimate is connected to every other physical
ultimate, in which case the universe *does* represent the maximally integrated
system.

In this essay, we have seen how it is possible to start with an experientially near anchor point—human consciousness, which we know without
doubt exists—and deduce that, in order to avoid conceptual incoherence as
well as conclusions that contradict what we have obtained from everyday
experience and bioscience, psyche divides into ego-mind, other-mind, and

matter. These three categories have complex relations that obtain in lawful and predictable ways. From these conclusions, along with a guiding principle of holism and preference for the experientially near over experientially far, we can deduce that mind *itself* is real, and derivative from a succession of greater wholes that expand further and further, on up to the universe itself. These "greater" (or at least more inclusive) minds have experience, qualia, and so forth in a way that we can only surmise is in some way similar to our own, since ours derive from them as part properties derive from whole properties. Because it embodies so much *more* matter, however, such trans-human systems are also likely difficult to imagine outside of visionary or parapsychological experiences.

This analysis answers question one (what is the origin of psyche?) by stating that psyche is brute, fully real, and possessed by the universe as a whole. Our second question (how do the categories of experience relate to one another?) we have answered by stating that the psyche of the universe is composed of numerous part-psyches (including our own), whose *local* psychic properties derive from that of the universal psyche by virtue of being the part of it that is viewed at this local level. We know about the cosmic consciousness only through the extrapolation of the fact that our own local psyche can itself be further decomposed into small sub-psyches whose properties derive from our own psyche—this flow of properties is required by the holism of the onto-phenomenological approach. That is, psyche is not "built up" from sub-psyches that create more expansive psyche *ex nihilo* (the pluralist approach). Rather, the properties of sub-psyches can be traced to the psyche of the larger system, and each decomposition, since it causes a reduction of integration, results in a loss of psychic scope and depth, until at the smallest level, there is minimal to no *local* psyche possessed by physical ultimates or unintegrated heaps beyond these heaps still always being part of the cosmic consciousness—of course, that aspect never changes. Put another way, we know the 100 billion neurons of the brain can possess local psyche *because of their integrateness as a whole*, but with each decomposition of it in which we cut off chunks of communication between the sub-systems, we lose local integratedness and reveal the smaller locally integrated sub-systems which were previously contributing to the larger local psyche of the whole. Since this works with human brains, it must continue to work with larger and more integrated systems "above" (i.e., of larger scope), on up to the cosmic consciousness. This arrangement and origin of psyche may seem bizarre to some, but it appears to be the only way to avoid the vexing problems created by pluralist approaches such as physicalism and micropsychism and the requirement for much more brute facts to account for what we already know exists—human psyche.

Thus, our second question is answered that psyche is a property of locally integrated matter, and both of them are fully real, but neither is truly derivative of one another. Both are, rather, derivative of the one entity from which all else is derived: the universe itself, which is composed of both matter and psyche. Which leads us to the third question (are the categories metaphysically separate or only conceptually and experientially separate?). Since in our formulation neither matter nor psyche are seen as prior, but part of a universal whole that is at the highest level complete and unified and free of distinction, we are reminded of the cosmology of the Neoplatonists (Plotinus, 1917, Proclus, 1963, Ficino, 2001). This ancient view states that all is derived from The One, itself all-encompassing and impossible to characterize without doing damage to it, but nevertheless containing "unity within multiplicity". In our modern terminology, the cosmos is composed of parts but the whole is always greater than the sum of those parts, so looking at the cosmos as anything other than a complete whole unto itself will always be ignoring the higher-order properties it possesses. Our holistic principle then can be seen as a restating of the Neoplatonic principle that all properties "emanate" from the One like rays from the sun. The difference between the ancient and modern approach, however, is that we are being more careful about how we arrive at the holistic principle, beginning with the experientially near human psyche and seeing if we can logically deduce, through admittedly abductive reasoning, at the originating principle, rather than simply stating it exists without justification and proceeding from there. The closest modern mind–body metaphysical position to this situation would be that of either neutral, dual, or multi-aspect monism that I have explored in more detail elsewhere (Goodwyn, 2019, 2020).

In any case, the holism of this macro-psyworld furthermore has required us to reconsider formal causes as fully real to account for the properties of some entities. I offer no defense of this maneuver other than that it allows us to evade the above conceptual quagmires (i.e. the physicalist problem, the combination problem, and the explosion of brute facts required to support the other positions), and so it may be worth accepting for this reason, but perhaps future work may help us to examine this more closely and justify it on other grounds. In any case, accounting for the origin of psyche as such, we might now make more progress on how to approach the concept of those elusive animals that live within the psyche: the archetypes. Though we have only thus far hinted at it, I believe archetypes will require us to examine the fourth type of causation, *final* causation.

References

Brentano, F. (1874 [1995]). The distinction between mental and physical phenomena. In Terrell, Rancurello and McAlister (Eds.), *Psychology from an Empirical Standpoint*. New York: Routledge.

Chalmers, D.J. (2016). The combination problem for panpsychism. In D. Chalmers (Ed.), *Panpsychism* (pp. 179–215). Cambridge: Oxford University Press.

Dennett, D.C. (1988). Quining qualia. In A. Marcel and E. Bisiach (Eds.), *Consciousness in Contemporary Science*. New York: Oxford University Press.

Ficino, M. (2001). *Platonic Theology*. Cambridge: Harvard University Press.

Goff, P. (2017). *Consciousness and Fundamental Reality*. Oxford: Oxford University Press.

Goodwyn, E. (2019). Jung and the mind-body problem. In J. Mills (Ed.), *Jung and Philosophy* (pp. 81–106). London: Routledge.

Goodwyn, E. (2020). Commentary on Mills' 'The Essence of Archetypes'. *International Journal of Jungian Studies* 12(2): 207–216.doi:10.1163/19409060-01201007.

Goodwyn, E. (2021a). Bodies and minds, heaps and syllables. *Synthese*, 199: 8831–8855. doi:10.1007/s11229-021-03184-7

Goodwyn, E. (2021b). Developing a metaphysical foundation for analytical psychology. In J. Mills (Ed.) *Psychoanalysis and the Mind Body Problem*. London: Routledge.

Mills, J. (2018). The essence of archetypes. *International Journal of Jungian Studies*, 10(3): 199–220.

Mills, J. (2020). Archetypal metaphysics and the psyworld. *International Journal of Jungian Studies*, 13(2): 130–149. doi:10.1163/19409060-bja10007.

Plotinus (1917/2007). *The Six Enneads of Plotinus*. New York: Forgotten Books.

Proclus (1963). *The Elements of Theology*. Oxford: Clarendon.

Schaffer, Jonathan (2010). Monism: The priority of the whole. *Philosophical Review*, 119: 31–76.

Chapter 7

Archetype, psyche, world

From experience to cosmopsychism

Jon Mills

There is nothing more intellectually entertaining, and challenging, than the question of metaphysics, as it is about the ultimate ground, cause, scale, and possibility of Being, existence, and reality, not all of which are necessarily the same. In his most recent essay on the origins of Psyche, Professor Erik Goodwyn offers the most ingenious erudite attempt to lay out a grand metaphysics of mind most philosophers would blush at, let alone endeavor. Since two minds often achieve more than one, let us see how far we can go in our continued dialogue to address some of these vexing, if not, irresolvable conundrums that continue to beset our metaphysical postulates on archetypes, psyche, and world.

In our series of exchanges (Goodwyn, 2020a,b, 2021; Mills, 2020a,b), we have engaged in constructive discourse on the ground, scope, and demarcations of archetypes and the broader conceptual parameters of what constitutes the psyche. Although we have been preoccupied with the question and nature of archetypes, our discussion has now brought us to engage the larger metaphysical delimitations of psyche and worldhood. As such, our projects are concerned with fundamental ontology and specifically the question of origins, namely, that which precedes in time and importance. The query of whether there is a *single* origin is the subject matter of Goodwyn's (2021) latest essay. It is akin to asking what is the origin of the universe, which implicitly evokes a divinity principle, namely, the single cosmogonic act of all creation: in a word, God.

Minding the mind

Goodwyn structures his investigation by asserting various ontological postulates, and then, following abductive inference, works them through to their logical conclusions. He starts with positing the existence of mind, which he equates with phenomenal experience on its most basal level, what he extends to consciousness and psyche, which I take to include all unconscious processes as well. From Descartes' *cogito*, Fichte's Absolute "I" (*Ich*) as pure self-posit, hence an act of self-assertion as the basis of psychic experience,

DOI: 10.4324/9781003349921-7

to Hegel's "I am I" as the truth of self-certainty, any mental activity presupposes a thinker as an extant being: anyone who denies this (Dennett, 1988) is intellectually disingenuous or simply performing mental masturbation out of amusement. Goodwyn seems to privilege consciousness when he speaks of Mind and experience, when I take consciousness and unconsciousness to be equiprimordial yet erupting from an underworld wellspring of unconscious experience (see Mills, 2010), the locus of archetypes. What we appear to agree upon is that what is most basic is experience itself—as act, as process, as event. But rather than use "mind," "experience," "consciousness," and "psyche" interchangeably, as Goodwyn does, I would tend to make hierarchical distinctions with Mind and Psyche being more robust complex organizations, whereas consciousness being a set of ordinal phenomenal properties belonging to Psyche, while unconscious experience being the basic building blocks of all mental processes.

We can even delineate experience into more descriptive functions and forms such as unconscious schemata, an archetype being one such schema. Yet, unconscious experience as schematic events are also simultaneously in communion with its own being, one I have argued initially exists as *prereflexive unconscious consciousness* (Mills, 2002a), a rudimentary subjectivity as a given simple presence, a presencing that becomes more present in experiential complexity and manifestation. So, even before experiential order can take shape unconsciously, let alone on macro-conscious levels of mind or psyche, experience and internal being are equivalent to *existence* itself, or more precisely, unconscious being-in-itself.

The ontological principle

Having prepared our discussion to include unconscious experience as a foundational starting point, Goodwyn centers on three conceptual divisions between self (ego), others (other minds), and world (matter) asking three further ontological questions, which I will reframe:

1 What is the ground from which entities derive?
2 What is their relation to one another?
3 Are they metaphysically separate or distinct from one another?

The first is the question of original ground, and more precisely, what is the ground that does the grounding for experience to arise? We are in agreement that there must be a derivative principle from which all else emerges and originates; and following question two, their *relationship* to one another is primordial, as we could not experience nor have communion with anything in the natural world without relatedness, for all experience is positional (relational). However, the questions still remain: How, what kind, and in what way? Following Goodwyn's third query—Are entities ontologically separate?—he is getting to the heart of the matter, pun intended. If mind or psyche, which for our purposes I will treat synonymously, is composed of experiential processes that coagulate and inhere in matter or our natural embodiment as psychic corporality, hence giving rise to consciousness, then the question becomes: Where does experience ultimately come from, or in other words, what is its cause?

From an onto-phenomenological framework, I have argued that unconscious experience is self-derived and self-constituted, arising from the rudimentary parameters of its initial natural interiority or psychic structure as an ontologically given process system. Goodwyn, on the other hand, asks an even more fundamental question: Where does Psyche ultimately come from? This leads him to posit a more primary or *pre-original* ground that he ultimately equates with the cosmos itself. But before we get there, and before my critique, it is important to show fidelity to Goodwyn's own method. He concludes that mind, objects, and matter indubitably exist, which we are in agreement, but he wants to explain how internal derivation (emergence) comes from the universe itself that is already derived and constituted, what we typically equate with reality, yet what he argues is simultaneously an enmattered psychic process system. If this is not a grand metaphysics, I don't know what would be.

Goodwyn is not satisfied with my conceptual limit (like Kant's *Ding-an-sich*, Fichte's *Anstoss*, or Husserl's *epoché*) or silence about where psyche comes from, as he sees this as tautological where "experiences come from themselves" despite avowing his proposition that mind exists. But we do agree that Psyche has ontological status and is real, so it becomes a matter of explaining how it is derived. "Where does all this come from?" he asks. Whereas I had confined my investigation to articulate how psyche and archetypes derive from unconscious process, Goodwyn asks us to venture into explaining how internal derivation is itself derived, hence either the psyche is (a) brute or given, or (b) "derives from something else." So ambitious in scope, I can hardly do justice to a thoughtful reply, as Goodwyn asks us to engage the ancient dilemma of *first cause*.

Following the ontological principle, we agree that something exists rather than nothing, albeit an ontology of nothingness may still exhibit metaphysical status as a realm of pure potentiality (the amorphous not-yet-realized), as absence, or more precisely, the presence of absence or lack, or as negation, for negation stands in dialectical relation to affirmation of being. Here, being and nothing could merely be the inverse of the same thing. But the point I wish to make is that we are starting with *something*, as mind and the material world simply don't just pop-up *ex nihilo*, unless one wants to qualify that the manifestation of the manifold of objects in the world come from a prior ground that must be its own grounding—an *ungrund* or ground without a ground, or we keep appealing to prior conditions, which inevitable leads us to an infinite regress. We can simply start from the premise that psyche *or* cosmos merely *is*—as the brute given, and bracket *how it got there*, instead focusing on how it is organized or constituted, as the question, Where does it derive? forces us down a rabbit hole. The question is akin to asking, Where does matter, space, and time come from? Regardless, we will be begging the question of *beginning* as the origin of origins. As the issue of first principles cannot be eluded, Goodwyn ventures out of the brackets and invites us along on his journey of attempting to answer how Psyche originates, a most admirable enterprise.

The matter of realism

As a proponent of metaphysical realism, namely, that an extant world exists independently from our minds or subjectivities, I believe that objects in the external world do not require our consciousness of them in order to exist. It is unclear if Goodwyn subscribes to this view, but he probably would concur. This means that the mind-independent nature and character of the world is not contingent upon our capacity to cognize it, therefore it is non-epistemic despite any correlation between subjectivity and the objective world.

Because we both situate our arguments within a naturalized framework, mine from our onto-phenomenal embodied existence, and his from physics and bioscience without succumbing to reductive scientific naturalism, I believe it is fair to say that we both endorse a generic realism that has two basic components: (1) existence, and (2) independence, namely, the universe (populated with objects) exists independent of any observer or mind required to sustain it. In this sense, the truth of what is real is non-epistemic, for an alethic premise of truth does not depend upon our capacity to recognize it. Therefore, the ontological conditions that make something true, and hence constitute the world, need not be knowable because they are verification-transcendent. In other words, the universe would be there no matter what without needing to be constituted by a subject. Furthermore, the world would not disappear if all finite observers or perceivers were to cease to exist. Although my experiences depend upon my psychic reality, cosmos or world does not. Put another way, mind is a necessary condition of our experience of the world but not a sufficient condition to explain the existence of the world that is independent of our minds. Hence realism becomes an inference to the *best* explanation.

Having clarified my metaphysical position, we may further discern another ontological feature of mind and world: we are part of nature. We find ourselves as natural organic objects within a naturalized cosmos despite having our own sense of autonomous existence as sentient conscious beings (subjects) that are nevertheless dependent upon our natural embodiment from which we are entangled and emerge as differentiated self-conscious minds.

On other minds

Goodwyn concludes that mind or psyche exists by deducing his own mind, and then through abduction, extends this postulate to the existence of other minds. His task to prove the existence of other minds may be addressed both empirically and practically in order to subvert the accusation of solipsistic illusion, yet this so-called classic problem in reality is a philosophical trope. By virtue of the fact that we relate to external objects that present as subjects with subjectivities similar to our own is sufficient enough to prove an inner relation to a mediated object even if it is merely a representation. The notion of solipsism is untenable as we cannot help but relate to objects in the natural world in which we find ourselves situated as part of our thrownness.

We detect the agency of other minds via mentalization, as no computer, artificial intelligence (AI), or robot has ever passed the Turing test, at least not yet. Hence we recognize ourselves in another's mind as having a separate existence despite having the shared capacity of consciousness. Given our empirical encounters with others similar to our own agency, it further becomes reasonable to presume a principle of subjective universality based on our experiential intersubjective relations to like-minded others, which allows us to reasonably deduce that minds exist independent of one's own personal psyche. This conclusion is brought forth most convincingly by Hegel (1807) in the *Phenomenology of Spirit* in his chapter on Self-Consciousness where the truth of one's own self-certainty is mediated by the recognition of "this other that presents itself to self-consciousness as an independent life,... a certainty which has become explicit for self-consciousness itself *in an objective manner* (*PS* § 174, p. 109, italics in original). Hence "self-consciousness is Desire": we see the Other's desire that exists independently from us, and like us, also *lacks* and *wants*. "A self-consciousness, in being an object, is just as much 'I' as 'object'. With this, we already have before us the Concept of *Mind*... 'I' that is 'We' and 'We' that is 'I'" (*PS* § 177, p. 110). What Hegel so nicely captures is the psychological process of being attuned to other's minds, what in contemporary psychoanalytic parlance has become known as mentalization—sensing the intentionality and inner conscious states of others' cognitive processes, and more specifically, *mentalized affectivity*.

We form a hypothesis or theory of other's minds by virtue of the fact that we encounter intersubjective relations in spacetime. In fact, in order to perceive or know that we have mental processes is mediated and confirmed by our relational encounters with others, as we must have a sense of self-certainty in order to identify and acknowledge that others do as well, or we would not be able to recognize our sense of self in the other as a separate existence (Mills, 2002a). This further allows us to construct a mental representation of what other minds must be like through identification and internalization of shared similarities and differences, or we would never be able to construct a meta-representational image of Otherness to begin with. First, we must respect the independence of the object (subject) as an autonomous being that has their own rich mental life experientially intuited and felt to be rationally deliberated by the mere fact that we sense they are reflecting on their own internal states of being. Since I am self-conscious of myself, I can readily see they are a self-conscious being as well engaging in cognitive, affective, and intentional (telic) reflective behaviors that are written on their embodied appearance (via body morphology, facial expressions, physical gestures, emotions, etc.). Here, we cannot elude the logical conclusion that our objects of consciousness are themselves somehow minded and have self-consciousness in their own right as an objective feature of reality or we would not be able to identify them as such in our experiences of the world. A failure to mentalize would leave us in a hopelessly self-enclosed universe that has no capacity to appreciate the objectivity of external reality and hence aborted to a monadic void. That is not how we experience the world of objects and others, as we are constantly relating to objects and others in our own mind. In other words, no objects, no mind.

The qualia of our convictions fortify our beliefs in the universality of mind due to the cognitive, perceptual, and affective resonance states they produce upon us in our relational encounters with others based on such agency detection mediated through our own agentic relation to self-interiority. What this further means is that deducing other minds requires an act of self-conscious awareness that recognizes the basis of subjectivity in self and others, for the inability to separate out different minds from one's own like we do with objects in the external world would result in some form of unconscious autism.

Minding matter

Professor Goodwyn is concerned with mereology and analyzes the part-to-whole relations between isolated objects and parts of the body as bits of matter that, when form in an assemblage, we often attribute to mind as a whole. In other words, human minds possess psyche while partitioned off components, our organs, let's say, do not; yet when combined into higher-order organizations, they constellate as mind. We may now ask: How do parts become mind? If we cannot answer how the lower relation informs and becomes subsumed within a higher causal order, we have a problem with mereological reduction on the one hand, and how autonomous teleological organization on a macro-system level is made possible on the other without reducing the whole to the sums of its parts. In order to address these concerns, Goodwyn alludes to two plausible possibilities: (1) all parts condition mind, and/or (2) parts are already proto-mental. This would mean they must either derive from something that is already psychic, or they become psychic when in synergy with an emergent complex process system.

Goodwyn states that when following an onto-phenomenological approach "'matter' is not given," when I have merely started from the empirical standpoint that psyche is embodied, therefore enmattered, hence is *given* just like our thrownness into worldhood. But Goodwyn does not want to beg the question of our enmattered psyche as a presupposition; he wants to explain how it is derived *and* how we get there, in other words, how we *become* psyche. His conclusion: "*mind is a property that is possessed by the matter of which I am composed.*" Because isolated bits of matter do not exhibit the attributes of local mindedness, mindedness is informed by isolated parts only in conjunction to a mental system as a whole.

If mind is a "property" of "matter," does matter do the possessing or does psyche possess matter? If matter possesses psyche, then are we not confronted with a reductive mereological fallacy, not to mention displacing the question of agency? In other words, if mind is an emergent property of matter, how could it have any causal powers of its own, as it only would be a causally impotent epiphenomenon? But if matter is itself psychic, the conundrum is eluded. Yet how is this possible?

I have been operating within a bracketed set of ontological assumptions that start from the phenomenal dialectical unfolding of psychic processes within mind or psyche itself as mediated interiority, while Goodwyn is hazarding out into speculative metaphysical waters that contemplates the ultimate origins of Psyche itself. Whereas I posit that the basic units of experience are constituted as unconscious micro-process systems unfolding and reconstituting as higher-order process systems of consciousness, Goodwyn challenges us to provide an account of how experience begins and where it derives from. It is not merely a matter of showing how experiential complexity of enmattered (concrete) process systems—viz. archetypes or unconscious schemata (in his language, local mindedness)—become more complex and convoluted in their higher modes of psychic organization. In order for mind to retain causal efficacy, we must be able to show how micro-process mental systems share the same properties and essence of all matter. And since we have agency, our own agency must derive from a source, or essence, whether that be single, simple, or complex is another matter, where all entities must participate even if they possess no agency.

The mind-body problem redux

Before Goodwyn arrives at his destination of offering us a metaphysics of psyche, he dismantles the classic problem of materialism by arguing that physicalism cannot provide an adequate account of the mindbody problem (MBP) for it cannot explain how matter creates psyche let alone justify its causally reductive ontology. Here, we are in agreement. We may further add the inconvenient irritant of a presupposed conceptual scheme that assumes mind and body are distinct: to accept matter vs. psyche is to enter into and confer a preestablished given binary, the very proposition of which is in question. Having already established that minds exist, Goodwyn then turns his attention to the question of panpsychism as an alternative to physicalism.

Cosmopsychism: plausibility and skepticism

Given that psyche exists, through inverse logic he challenges the materialist paradigm that takes as brute fact the physical existence of the universe in the absence of psyche, which he questions as the ground or cause of mind. Rather, he proceeds with the premise that psyche exists and tries to account for matter as either a creation or co-extension of psyche. He opines: "Because psyche (or proto-psyche) already exists everywhere to one degree or another, there is no need to give any explanation for how matter creates it. It is simply a property that exists in the universe that is possessed by some or all of said universe." But this commitment immediately lands him into hot water, which he acknowledges. If we can't convincingly establish that matter creates mind, then how about the other way around? But the same problem applies: you have to account for how psyche creates or coalesces matter if you posit it as the original cause. One option is to look at micro-panpsychic processes that then scale up to macro-organizations at the systemic level. Here, panpsychism starts with the minute building blocks of the universe that are posited to be micropsychic and hence inform the bigger system, namely, one big macropsyche. But the same quandary reiterates itself that the physicalists face: in similar vein as the difficulty in explaining how micro-bits of matter create mind, how can tiny micropsyches come together to form one big universe animated as consciousness?

Goodwyn's solution: *cosmopsychism*—"the framework that proposes that the entire universe possesses consciousness" right down to atoms, electrons, and quarks. He argues that if we start with the whole as a system, we may then more readily infer how parts, subunits, or isolated bits of matter may be modifications or derivatives of the whole. Therefore, we are less likely to run into logical contradiction if the whole of the universe is posited as possessing psyche that then modifies itself and differentiates itself into parts or objects that would still retain the essence and properties of the whole in dispersed derivative forms. Mind may be explained as its own whole, which is a subsystem or altered form of the cosmos. A quantum particle is a further modification of universal mind on the most minute level of consciousness. Because every modification is the extension and stratification of Psyche's original essence, all objects and properties of the universe are strewn into a plurality of entities that retain their relation to the original unity. Goodwyn believes this eliminates the combination problem of explaining how both physicalist and micropsychic processes are said to emerge and create a macro-organization that scales up to create the whole as an aggregate mental apparatus. By starting with the whole—what we find ourselves emersed in as mind, society, and cosmos, or in my language, psyworld, Goodwyn asks us to adopt panpsychism as a viable solution to the MBP and the greater metaphysical constraints that condition the real through cosmogonic ontology.

Before I critique Goodwyn's position by adopting the onto-phenomenological method that starts with experience-near phenomena while extending such or-dinal phenomenology beyond the human psyche to the cosmos as a whole, we must revisit how this challenges our views on metaphysical realism. Previously we argued that there is a universe that exists independent of our minds that cognize it, and there are no epistemic criteria required to maintain the extant world as its own autonomous ontological reality. But, if the whole cosmos is psychic, metaphysical realism becomes compromised. If one adopts any ver-sion of panpsychism, this confounds the notion of realism as there would no longer be independent existence of anything from Mind for all of reality would be relegated to the psychic. This would by default make our realist claims some version of an anti-realist metaphysics or subsumed within some form of Idealism. How can the world exist independent of mind, hence evoking the ontological principle of metaphysical realism, when the universe to some de-gree possesses psychic processes? This means that there is nothing that exists independent of psyche, as all matter is infused with consciousness, and pre-sumably must be so necessarily in order to sustain the real. *Ergo* there is noth-ing independent of mental processes that saturate the cosmos. Is there a way out of this pickle? Let us see how far we get before arriving at any definitive conclusions.

The merit of Goodwyn's theory is that it solves the logical problem of ac-counting for essence: nothing is completely estranged from the objects that saturate the universe because everything is a modification from an original source that is predicated on a Whole or philosophy of the Encompassing. Instead of starting with isolated bits of matter that form into particular arrangements and assemblances that become further organized into con-sciousness or psyche, hence the hard problem of neuroscience, Goodwyn starts with an organic whole and then works backwards toward understand-ing how parts or constituencies are distributed forms of essence into mi-croprocesses that are extensions of a mature system. From a philosophy of organism where an onto-phenomenology unfolds, in my thinking I begin with the micropsychic, what I call microagency, that then developmentally progresses into more robust forms of unconscious subjectivity that then breach into consciousness, thereby relying upon a dialectical logic of subla-tion where lower relations volute and are subsumed into higher ones as an organism acquires new forms of sophistication in its developmental helices. Here, essence is basic to the most primitive as well as the more mature forms psyche assumes. Because I am working from the inside-out, I attempt to provide a framework where psyche emerges from the base material in which it finds its nascent self situated as embodied desire. In my system, psyche simply does not emerge *ex nihilo*, a point Goodwyn may have confounded, but is developmentally prepared through incremental forms of dialectical volution that organize into higher topographies of psychic evolution. The rudimentary given is already a microprocess that matures into an organic mental whole we call mind or psyche. Essence is diffused internally until it breaches externality, namely, the manifold of objects it encounters in consciousness.

Goodwyn's method is different: he jumps to the end and works his way back, where the whole explains how modified constituent parts may be understood to exist as emanations or dispersions from the mature organism in question. But, here is the leap. Goodwyn does not confine this metaphysic to the human psyche or as a society of collective peoples, but rather extends to the whole cosmos itself as one enormous animating consciousness where everything else is derived.

Let us proceed with some paradoxical or aporic questions. *How can the universe ponder itself?* How can the cosmos think itself, let alone have self-consciousness as an experientially aware entity that thinks? How can it think itself into being? Here, we cannot escape the specter of supernaturalism or appeal to a divinity principle, as a psychic cosmos has generative powers to confer being onto other things through virtue of its capacity to dispense its essence into distributive forms and patterns throughout the universe including inanimate objects and animal bodies. And if plausible arguments can be given to defend these propositions, you still have to explain how *Cosmopsyche* came into existence as a cosmogonic act. And does this not beg the question of first cause? Here, we fall into a black hole of infinite regress. So, we must contend with the predicate that the universe has always existed in some form despite undergoing transmogrification as a processual system of the whole, or we must be prepared to tackle how a universe emerged or came into being as a psychic system. Regardless, we are back to the question of fundamental ontology—What is the origin of Being?

How did consciousness magically get there in the cosmos to begin with as Universal Mind? It presupposes the very thing in need of explication as it presumes consciousness is everywhere, but it does not explain consciousness nor how it got there originally. To answer this, it bears repeating, we are either back to infinite regression, or we have to appeal to a creative function, divinity principle, or that the universe is eternal, infinite, and was never created—it was merely always there *qua* Being. So here, Goodwyn is in the same quagmire I am when having to start with the brute given: while I appeal to embodied immediacy, he postulates a supraordinate source of all consciousness as the universe itself. I would argue I am on more stable ground by instituting the ontological bracket, but this does not answer to the greater metaphysical questions Goodwyn astutely raises.

Transcendental heavens

Is Professor Goodwyn justified in extending his notion of psychic holism that is peculiar to human beings to the cosmos itself? Why should we assume Cosmopsyche exists as something that is brute structuring and suffusing the whole heavens when this may easily slide into theosophy where cosmos becomes the mind of God? Why not stay within the parameters of the human rather than superhuman, or conversely, simply make Psyche a generic abstraction or development of the universe? If we have the continued problem of not being able to adequately explain what consciousness is, which enjoys no uniform consensus, let alone how it arises, how are we any better off by importing consciousness to the physical universe where both psyche and matter are said to form an integrated unit? I cannot solve the matter of first cause, for, as previously stated, it either leads to infinite regression, circularity, begging the question, and/or the inevitable bog of antinomies that meet with no resolution, sublation, or discernible synthesis. But may I indulge the very questions that beset a grand metaphysics of inclusion required to justify a theory of holism cosmopsychism is said to afford?

How can distinct subjectivities belonging to distinct minds of individuals tally up to be combined in a single conscious Mind? Here, the combination problem leads to incoherence because, by definition, if my mind derives from the One Big Mind holding everything together through interconnectedness, I should be able, in theory, to be in communion with every subject's consciousness as well as the Big Kahuna's. Since I am hardly aware of all aspects of my own mind, how could I be said to possess access to other's minds, let alone the properties, qualia, and viewpoints of all existing beings on the planet and throughout the galaxies, which is empirically unverifiable and logically impossible, therefore contradictory and incoherent? But Goodwyn offers us a potential explanation. Although the properties of micropsyches may be traced to the larger system and integrated within the whole, they lose their local integratedness when partitioned off into subsystems or units, and therefore this accounts for why parts of the whole system lose direct communication with one another, as they are alienated and discrete entities in their own right despite remaining in communion with the one large Unity as particulars within the universal that it emanates from. For Goodwyn, if I understand him correctly, psyche is neither derived from matter nor is matter derived from psyche, as they are both co-extensive within a synchronized concomitant system whereby psyche inheres in matter and vice versa; yet this locally integrated psychic matter (and energy) ultimately derives from one entity, namely, the universe itself. Here, Goodwyn succeeds in providing a reasonable argument that may account for how the binary categories of psyche and matter are fused in a concurrent co-system without privileging one as derivative of the other. Let's call this *psymatter* as shorthand for our psychic embodiment. But what about the cogency of prioritizing the premise and metaphysical status of the One from which all things derive?

By attributing an Über-Mind to the cosmos itself, Goodwyn is looking for the ultimate foundation in which *all things arise* and engage through a participatory metaphysics when I merely confine my investigation to the human psyche. The problems are enormous when attributing thought, consciousness, and psychological processes to an impersonal universe composed of a multiplicity of objects that are said to possess *cognition* that are differentiated yet further integrated or unified in the One. To reiterate, the most salient questions that draw into question the dubiousness of such claims come to mind. As previously stated, how can the universe *think*? How can it conceive of itself at all? How can it *imagine*? How can it *feel*? How can it be conscious of itself, hence self-aware? This would imply having self-consciousness and its own agency, especially if everything else that is extant is contingent and dependent upon the One's own being and actions that sustain all the bits and pieces of the cosmos through dispersion of its essence. And how could it scatter itself into other objects and subjects that populate the universe? What are the mechanics involved? Does it do so *conceptually*, through thought, or *physically* through the materialization of substance-energy-matter? Does it *create* an infinite sea of miniobjects that possess psymatter, or does it merely rearrange and allocate already existing psymatter in new and variegated forms? And what would be its motivations for doing so? In short, how could the universe possess *soul* let alone be the cause—the ultimate ground—of other souls?

One attempt to address these aporias, albeit with their own set of problematics, is if we were to redefine what we typically mean by *consciousness*. Here, Whitehead may prove to be instructive. Like Goodwyn, Whitehead (1925, 1929) proposes a philosophy of organism where reality is a holistic encompassing process system composed of basic drops of experience that saturate all objects, what he calls actual occasions or actual entities, that are related to everything in the universe through an interconnected ontic web of prehensions as concrescing occasions. Everything that exists or is actual has an elementary mind-like structure that scales up in aggregate form to the Whole as the nontemporal concrescence of all actual occasions that unifies and holds the cosmos together (Mills, 2002b). Although Whitehead goes to great lengths to distance himself from the language of consciousness and panpsychism, unconvincingly so, he also imports psychological properties and qualia to actual entities in the form of desire, feelings, and subjectivity, a deposit of the limits of human language in trying to articulate the internal dynamics of the manifold in relation to (and belonging to) a cosmogonic ontology. In this way, the universe is alive and teaming with energies but it is not entirely animate in the same manner as animal bodies, because different gradations of consciousness are posited to manifest differently, quantitatively and qualitatively, in different process systems and in different hierarchical societies (Mills, 2003). We know these basic vital processes exist thanks to modern physics and bioscience but are explained through different paradigms and semantic discourses. So, following Goodwyn, what is foundational is the essence of *form* as a process system however which way we wish to characterize it, the details of which are mute. But this brings us full circle back to the question of archetypes as a derivation of original form. Although Goodwyn looks to science and physics, even contemplating the universe being entangled at the quantum level, he would be among good company with Whitehead.

Professor Goodwyn (2021) summaries his conclusions and theses in the following manner:

> In our modern terminology, the cosmos is composed of parts but the whole is always greater than the sum of its parts, so looking at the cosmos as anything other than a complete whole unto itself will always be ignoring the higher-order properties it possesses. Our holistic principle then can be seen as a restating of the Neoplatonic principle that all properties 'emanate' from the One like rays from the sun. The difference between the ancient and modern approach, however, is that we are being more careful about how we arrive at the holistic principle, beginning with the experientially near human psyche and seeing if we can logically deduce, through admittedly abductive reasoning, the originating principle, rather than simply stating it exists without justification and proceeding from there.

Goodwyn's logic is internally consistent and in many ways persuasive. But what happens if we don't buy into the premise that there is an ultimate "originating principle" and that there is simply a plurality of objects that constitute the cosmos that has always been infinite (*Ananta*) and uncaused, such as in the Vedic tradition or its permutation as the *Ein Sof* in Kabbalah? How can something be a "complete whole" when everything is in flux and is a process of becoming? What if the universe is nothing but multiplicity and particularity that are subsumed under a unity principle but are never unified, such as a container or cipher? What if holism is merely a semantic signifier for totality, hence a symbolic Absolute without the need to import entirety, finality, closure, its completion and end? What if we do not concede that holism exists as an original metaphysical unity and instead are conditioned to seek unification and integration by virtue of reason in order to make sense of things rather than participating of or seeking a return to an originating symbiosis with a universal Source? What if the psychology of unitive thinking and the need for a "holistic principle" is based on the human desire for wholeness, peace, and merger with the *notion* of the ultimate, infinity, or God, rather than there truly being an actuality of Oneness?

More metaphysical baggage

Does the notion that everything derives from a holistic cosmic mind hold any water? Is this the ingenuity of creative imagination—merely a fantasy, the cunning of reason? It is hard to deny that if we accept these premises, our speculations on the mental may lead us down a Jungian path into the mystic. Goodwyn's turn to Neoplatonism comes with its own metaphysical baggage, as it presupposes and is committed to a first principle of (a) the One (*hen*) as a preordained Whole, which is ultimately conditioned and sustained by (b) a Divinity Principle or Godhead. The former proceeds from a philosophy of containment or encapsulation that spreads out through hierarchical derivation into processions or emanations of entities with their own series of metaphysical layers into a graded reality that come from the Source (first principle), which remains ineffable yet is connected and internal to the human soul through intellection and divinization (theurgy) practices (see Plotinus, *Enneads*; Proclus, *Elements of Theology*; Remes, 2008). This roughly corresponds to Goodwyn's scheme that makes the human mind derivative of the cosmos or universe. Despite my earlier reservations, this system of thought may be potentially compatible with metaphysical realism that espouses the belief in a mind independent reality that is simultaneously represented in mind by virtue of our shared essence, a conceptual move that was later adopted in Schelling's and Hegel's *Naturphilosophie* where mind as subject –object identity is seen as an organic development of nature. But, there is a problem. How do we account for the one and the many?

Beginning with the premise from Parmenides that being itself is one, Plotinus initiates his treatise on the "philosophy of the One" (*Enneads*, VI.9[9].3.14) in the following fashion:

> It is by the One that all beings are being, both those which are primarily being and those which are in any sense said to be amongst beings. For what could anything be if it were not one? For if things are deprived of the One which is predicated of them, they are not those things.
>
> *Enneads*, VI.9[9].1.1-4

Here, One is a unity of singularity that conditions all being. Singularity as unitarity is the essence of anything that exists, as the existence of all things is being. Yet, the One is indivisible and is the original cause of being. There is no division, no separation, no difference within pure identity. It embraces a simplicity thesis of the rudimentary presence of identity where everything is collapsed into solitariness. The solitary is also further intimately connected to the notion of nothingness as "that which is not one (*oude hen*)" (Plato, *Republic*, 478b), which Plotinus espouses (*Enneads*, V.2[11].1.1). Only one exists or it is nothing (*ouden*).

Unity is essence and essence in-itself is unified, hence being the basis of all Being. Unity is foundational to everything, both ontologically and episte-mologically. For the Neoplatonists, all that exists—the many—is contingent upon the one as an unconditioned unity that conditions all unity (*Enneads*, V.3[49].15.12–14). And since all unity must be a united multiplicity within a unified whole, the whole itself is comprised of *unities* as its totality. There-fore, multiplicity is unified with the whole as "the unity of the totality of a multiplicity, just as much as the unity of each one of its individual compo-nents" (Halfwassen, 2014, p. 183). Without opposition, beyond all otherness, as the ground and source of all existence that transcends difference, the One is Absolute (*apolyton*) (*Enneads*, VI.8[39].20.6). Ultimately we are one, and the loneliest one at that, because nothing can exist other than a featureless sterile totality. If this is the case it is hardly worthy of worship when all sin-gularity vanishes into singularity, like the manner in which Plotinus ends his ninth tractate of the final ennead, as "the passing of solitary to solitary."

Goodwyn's adoption of Neoplatonic holism commits him to the con-clusion that the One transcends yet conditions everything as the ordering principle to all Being and is the ultimate explanation of all reality. A stand-ard criticism of Neoplatonic metaphysics is that because it posits the One as a transcendent unity, which exists *before* and *beyond* being itself, it is not able to maintain its relation to the derivation of all things as gradations of reality because it exceeds all things. The problem of the one and the many is that the One by definition is unchanging and lacks differentiation, multiplicity, and the attributes of being because it is conceived as a com-plete and holistic identity while at the same time is said to be the source of the multiplicity of beings. Put laconically, how can all things be from the One when it is estranged from the particular beings in which all things are said to derive and participate? The predicate as principle contradicts itself. Here, we have the same problem with panentheism and natural theology that boasts the cosmological argument for the existence of God. The One becomes the Wizard of Oz behind the curtain that is supposed to be cur-tainless. In other words, there are no appearances in absolute singularity. All there is is one.

The transcendence of the One is an obstacle to a participatory metaphys-ics as it remains isolated from all beings in which it is said to commune. So, either the multiplicity of beings must reside within the One or the One creates the universe of objects that reside outside of its internal structure. The former violates the principle of simplicity of the whole where there is no multiplicity, differentiation, or attributes of objects and the latter violates the notion of monism as shared essence. If something is in the One, then it is not one as any distinctions shatter its primal unity. If something is one it is simply one, not many. And if there are derivations, gradations, and hi-erophanies of reality that are caused by the One, then how can these lesser realities be tantamount to the One? As Sara Ahbel-Rappe (2014) puts it, "how can absolute unity give rise to multiplicity in the first place?" (p.168). The problem lies in its transcendence as crypto-theology.

The overarching question of psyche in Jung's system

It is beyond the scope of this project to offer a defense of Neoplatonism, for I simply wanted to highlight these ancient preoccupations and problematics. The question now becomes: How does all of this relate to analytical psychology? Applying Goodwyn's logical scheme that the human psyche derives from a cosmic Psyche, like Jung's notion of the Objective Psyche, the collective unconscious becomes the bedrock of the universe animated by the cosmos *operating unconsciously*. This is an important point to make, as we do not witness nor experience the cosmic psyche, that is, as having its own mind like we experience other people to have minds, yet through our internal relation to externality the world manifests *in* us. We are in psyche; we are psyworld. Here, psyche is its own cosmos, a mirror of the whole. Our individual subjectivities are merely a particularity, an instance of one of the multiplicities of Neoplatonic metaphysics, one within one.

How are we connected to this collective unconscious? Because it manifests as the appearance of *patterned form* in all people regardless of time, place, culture, or peculiarity of our thrownness, namely, as archetypes. Cosmos awakens psyche, where we find ourselves as particularity within universality, as an encapsulated multiverse of the mind. Deep down we all likely experience some primal unity with the cosmos, no matter how faint, amorphous, or ill-defined, as it presents itself to us as primordial presence, totality, ineffability, wonder. In mereological terms, we are part of the whole.

Following a Jungian trajectory, the collective psyche releases its essence into archetypes that resurface in the minds of humans. They are eternal, as is the process of essence distribution. In Neoplatonic fashion, this objective psyche is the whole that establishes the array of psyches that constitute social collectives, what I have previously interpreted as emanations that "supervene" on our individualistic minds and subjective personalities (Mills, 2014). Archetypes are the primal forms instantiated within mind while the collective unconscious is the transcendental transpersonal field holding all psyches together through shared universality.

What may be more radical than attributing consciousness to the cosmos is the notion that *the cosmos is unconscious*. Given that modern physics tell us that approximately 95% of the universe is comprised of dark matter and dark energy clouded by the Higgs field that has never manifested, perhaps this is not such a farfetched concoction. If 95% of what is postulated to exist has never materialized nor been directly observed, it not only remains unconscious and unknown, it is believed to condition all of reality in every region of the universe. Yet it remains hidden. And anything hidden is the ultimate form of unconsciousness.

Perhaps the cosmic unconscious speaks to us indirectly, as something revealed yet concealed unconsciously, the intuition and emotional resonance of the need to merge with Origin as the desire for transcendence. To bathe in the primal source, our pure spirit and true home, eternal return; may we be at peace with God as the tensionless state of being one.

But aren't we now engaging in psychomythology as a transference to theory? In previous work (Mills, 2019), I have argued that the collective unconscious is merely a synecdoche for universality, or more specifically, a subjective universality that is part of all human minds as collective objectivity. There is no need to import a supernatural hypostasis as the cause and creator behind the scenes. Archetypes may be explained through naturalized psychology that both Professor Goodwyn and I have attempted to accomplish, each in our own ways. Do we need to take this next leap of faith to allot psyche to the universe to reasonably expatiate what we know about the human mind? Although I applaud his efforts to resolve the riddle of Being, I will leave it for others to decide such plausibility. In the end, we have both advanced an onto-phenomenology underlying various metaphysical assumptions about mind and cosmos that are integral to Jungian theory. I hope these new directions in analytical psychology lead to new research and developing insights that continue to shed light on the notions of archetype, psyche, and world.

References

Ahbel-Rappe, S. (2014). Metaphysics: The origin of becoming and the resolution of ignorance. In P. Remes and S. Slavea-Griffin (Eds.), *The Routledge Handbook of Neoplatonism* (pp. 166–181). London: Routledge.

Dennett, D.C. (1988). Quining qualia. In A. Marcel and E. Bisiach (Eds.), *Consciousness in Contemporary Science*. Oxford: Oxford University Press.

Goodwyn, E. (2020a). Archetypal origins: Biology vs culture is a false dichotomy. *International Journal of Jungian Studies*, 13(2): 111–129.

Goodwyn, E. (2020b). Commentary on Mills' "The Essence of Archetypes." *International Journal of Jungian Studies*, 12(2): 207–216.

Goodwyn, E. (2021). The origins of psyche: From experience to ontology. *International Journal of Jungian Studies*, 13(2). Published online.

Halfwassen, J. (2014). The Metaphysics of the one. In P. Remes and S. Slavea-Griffin (Eds.), *The Routledge Handbook of Neoplatonism* (pp. 182–199). London: Routledge.

Hegel, G.W.F. (1807). *Phenomenology of Spirit*. A.V. Miller (Trans.), 1977. Oxford: Oxford University Press.

Mills, J. (2002a). *The Unconscious Abyss: Hegel's Anticipation of Psychoanalysis*. Albany, NY: State University of New York Press.

Mills, J. (2002b). Whitehead idealized: A naturalized process metaphysics. *Process Studies*, 31(1): 32–48.

Mills, J. (2003). Whitehead's unconscious ontology. *Theory & Psychology*, 13(2): 209–238.

Mills, J. (2010). *Origins: On the Genesis of Psychic Reality*. Montreal: McGill-Queens University Press.

Mills, J. (2014). *Underworlds: Philosophies of the Unconscious from Psychoanalysis to Metaphysics*. London: Routledge.

Mills, J. (2019). The myth of the collective unconscious. *Journal of the History of the Behavioral Sciences*, 55(1): 40–53.

Mills, J. (2020a). Archetypal metaphysics and the psyworld. *International Journal of Jungian Studies*. 13(2): 130–149. doi:10.1163/19409060-bja10007

Mills, J. (2020b). On the origins of archetypes. *International Journal of Jungian Studies*, 12(2): 201–206.

Plato (1961). Republic. In E. Hamilton and H. Cairns (Eds.) *The Collected Dialogues of Plato* (pp. 575–844). Princeton, NJ: Princeton University Press.

Plotinus (1966). *Enneads*. A.H. Armstrong (Trans. & Comm.). Cambridge, MA: Harvard University Press.

Proclus (1963). *Elements of Theology*. E.R. Dodds (Trans. & Comm.), 2004. Oxford: Clarendon Press.

Remes, P. (2008). *Neoplatonism*. London: Routledge.

Whitehead, A.N. (1925). *Science and the Modern World*. New York: Macmillan/Free Press.

Whitehead, A.N. (1929). *Process and Reality*. Corrected Edition, D.R. Griffin & D.W. Sherburne (Eds.), 1978. New York: Free Press.

Chapter 8

Psyche, world, archetype
Final thoughts

Erik Goodwyn

Conscious and unconsciousness

I wanted to cover a few minor points before getting to the main content. First, when discussing my view of the origins of psyche, I did not mention the distinction between conscious and unconscious psychic content. Rather, I focused on qualia. The reason is that qualia are undeniably extant—they provide the anchor point for my analysis. That unconscious processes occur, I have no doubt, but they must be secondarily inferred from the analysis of what is conscious. By definition, unconscious processes are not available to immediate awareness, therefore there can be no other way to arrive at them other than through extrapolating their necessity via meticulous study of the mind and brain. Nevertheless, I essentially agree with Mills' characterization of consciousness arising from a multilayered and complex unconscious evolution of content. More on this later.

Metaphysical realism into holistic panpsychism

Mills' (2022) critique of metaphysical realism as it applies to my model requires some comment. I am not necessarily committed to the reality of a non-psychic world that is independent of psyche in general, just a world that is independent of *my own* psyche. Ultimately the position of holistic panpsychism (one variant of which is cosmopsychism) is one in which the maximally conscious entity—possibly the universe itself—as a coherent whole unto itself possesses the property of consciousness, from which all other consciousnesses are derived as parts of that whole. This particular way of looking at the mind–body relation is *monistic* in the sense that psyche is not seen to be a separate substance from matter. Rather, matter composes the parts of the holistic form that possesses the property of consciousness. This matter itself possesses psyche in its measure, too (because it derives from the whole that has it), only it is progressively more primitive and unconscious the more *relatively dis-integrated* it is. The more you break up the cosmic consciousness, the more limited and unconscious that piece of relatively un-integrated psyche is. The key difference is the holism—meaning

DOI: 10.4324/9781003349921-8

the place we look to explain consciousness. The holist, unlike the plural-ist, does not believe that any holistic property such as consciousness can derive from the properties of its parts *even in principle* because wholes are ontologically prior to parts. Since pluralism is so often assumed without ac-knowledgement, this is often the point at which others get tripped up by this position. But, it is the common element embedded in *all* the classic mind–body problems that have stymied attempts to explain consciousness up to this point. The "hard problem" of consciousness, the binding problem of neuroscience, even the combination problem of (micro-) panpsychism are all pluralist at heart, and it wasn't until I read the work of 15th century Neoplatonist Marsilio Ficino (2001) that I realized there was an ancient an-swer to these issues. Ficino's analysis is somewhat quaint in comparison to the modern versions of such analyses, but it nevertheless contains the key ingredient needed to resolve the mind–body problem in my opinion: holistic mereology.

That starting point, combined with the insights of over a century of modern philosophy of mind as well as tremendous progress in neurosci-ence led me to this position: we know from neuroscience that *integrated wholes* are forms which consistently possess consciousness (i.e., the frontal cortices, when they are attached to a human body, the consciousness of other animals). Hence, there is no known reason (outside of clinging to some kind of vitalism) that larger wholes that are maximally integrated in a similar way wouldn't also, though these are currently unavailable for direct study unfortunately, and the *characteristics* of such consciousness might be quite alien to our experience (but for some preliminary work on that subject, see Sloman, et al., 2021). Such systems of matter would include populations of humans, ecosystems, the biosphere, on up to pro-gressively more inclusive systems such as galaxies and possibly even the entire universe.

This idea undoubtedly might sound a little bonkers—at least to mod-ern readers. But it's actually an extremely old idea, the core of which—panpsychism—has enjoyed something of a renaissance in the last few decades, slowly eroding the dominant hard-core physicalism of the last cen-tury (Kelly and Kelly, 2009; Koons and Bealer, 2010).

My full defense of one particular type of panpsychism—holistic cosmopsychism-—can be found elsewhere (Goodwyn, 2021), but others such as d'Espagnat (2006), Goff (2017), Keppler and Shani (2020), Shani (2015), and Vazza (2017) have explored its merits before me. What I have added to the conversation is a commitment to holistic mereology. Again—nothing new with this, it's just that such holism, up until recently (Schaf-fer 2010), has been unpopular within the philosophical Zeitgeist just as any anti-physicalism. An ancient example of such a strongly holistic system would be Neoplatonism.

Neoplatonism and the separateness of the whole from its parts

Neoplatonism leads me to the main content of my reply. The various objections to Neoplatonism that Mills reviews appear to be stuck at one central issue—how can the One contain multiplicity yet remain itself singular/simple? Perhaps it is easier to imagine the answer to this by using a smaller whole: that of a human being, since it is far closer to our experience.

To ask how the One can be whole and complete, singular and yet still containing multiplicity within it, we need look no further than our own bodies. One hundred billion neurons, each isolated in its own petri dish, sitting next to a body does not a human make. Only when those neurons are arranged *just so* and furthermore attached in a specific way to a body with its concomitant organs does one observe a self, complete with qualia of color, sound, music, feeling, poetry, taste, and panache. The mind–body problem asks just this: *how does this miracle occur? Why does merely sticking them together conjure up subjective qualia—something seemingly very different from isolated biomolecules, and are themselves undeniably real?*

Before we see how this relates to the Neoplatonic worldview, let's review the three common answers to this question:

1   The neurons and other cells somehow *causally generate* the psyche of the human to appear where there was none, though we have no idea how (physicalism).
2   The neurons all have their own little micropsyches and when they start interacting, somehow the macropsyche of the human appears, though we have no idea how (micropsychism).
3   Neurons and other cells may have their own micropsyches, but they don't create the macropsyche—rather, bringing the neurons and other cells together into the proper *form* is what formally causes the macropsyche to emerge. This form possesses psyche because it is part of the Ultimate psychic Form—a theoretical construct that represents the most integrated whole form that is possible. (holistic panpsychism, one possible conclusion of which is cosmopsychism).

Unlike the first two, the third does not require a miracle to happen—i.e., does not require brute emergence. Mills' description of the emergence of consciousness elucidates very clearly how all this looks from the "inside", meaning as the human body gets closer and closer to the *form* needed to possess consciousness. Where we differ is in how we want to try to incorporate matter. We know matter exists and we know consciousness exists. For Mills, that is enough, and that is fair. But my own biomedical background forces me to go farther, if I can. More on this momentarily.

Sensing this, Mills (2022) asks:

> If mind is a 'property' of 'matter', does matter do the possessing or does psyche possess matter? If matter possesses psyche, then are we not confronted with a reductive mereological fallacy, not to mention displacing the question of agency? In other words, if mind is an emergent property of matter, how could it have any causal powers of its own?).

He then goes on to provide some good reasons not to take the Neoplatonic analogy too far with some quotes from the *Enneads*. And it is not my intention to make a full-blown defense of classical Neoplatonism here—I meant only to observe the similarities between the ancient view and what my own current model arrives at, and recognize the inspirations for my proposed solution. Nevertheless, I do think some conceptual work can be done with the objections Mills calls attention to: that of the independence/transcendence of the One and the seeming contradiction embedded in the idea that it could simultaneously be simple and undivided and yet *also* contain multiplicity within it. My defense of this idea comes by way of mereological analysis of things far closer to us than the cosmos—everyday things that are wholes with parts. The cosmopsychism is merely the result of taking these everyday observations to their logical conclusion.

Music

I return to the analogy of a piece of music to illustrate the way I think mind and matter are related as parts are to (certain kinds of) wholes. A melody is a collection of notes that, in the hands of an artful composer, creates a phrase that has a feeling that is unique to it. I used the example of the famous "Ode to Joy" melody written by Beethoven for his Ninth Symphony. The properties of this melody—its particular contours, feeling, and character—do not derive from the notes themselves but by the particular way in which they are arranged, i.e., by the *form* of the notes. The melody, as a unit, has a property of its own that does not belong to any of the notes in particular, even though you could not write a melody without notes. To bring us back to matter and mind, then, the answer is similar: like notes, individual bits of matter isolated from one another do not possess the kind of psyche observed by bits of matter *arranged and connected just-so*. The larger, arranged-just-so psyche, in this sense, transcends the matter, just as the melody transcends the notes—especially when you take into consideration the fact that more than one arrangement of matter can correlate with the same gestalt feeling/experience/quale. Like statues of Zeus, neither lumps of marble nor bronze contain Zeus-ness. But either can be arranged to produce a statue that has the property of Zeus-ness. Similarly, melody must not only transcend notes but also must contain them. The statue of Zeus is a form which transcends the particular material it is made of, but it nevertheless requires material anyway. Psyche transcends the cells arranged into a body and brain, but still requires them. Psyche, then, is *formally caused*, not materially caused. Expecting psyche to be materially caused would be to defend vitalism, for which no good evidence exists—frankly it shocks me how few investigators realize this. In any case, the lessons of the various quagmires of philosophy of mind (i.e, the hard problem, binding problem, and combination problems), however, teach us that psyche is also not merely *efficiently* caused either—we will get to this latter point later.

Sound

To further clarify, let's look at sound quales. When air molecules vibrate in compression waves, they impinge upon the eardrum, and this sets up a chain reaction through the middle and inner ear to cause fibers of the auditory system to fire in a particular way. And yet, none of that is experienced by the subject—instead, we "hear a sound". This sound is furthermore not an "illusion" but an undeniable quale. Some day we may achieve a perfect understanding of how each particular pattern of auditory nerve firings *correlate* with each particular sound (and, as mentioned, do not be fooled into thinking this is a one-to-one process; I am ignoring the issue that two patterns may correlate with the same sound and/or the same pattern can correlate with different sounds in different environmental conditions—all of these variants have been observed by neuroscience). Nevertheless, what is missing here is the explanation as to *why* pattern X *sounds precisely the way it does and not some other way.* We have absolutely no way of answering this question via physicalism. In fact, we don't even know *how* we could determine it (and, of course, micropsychism fares no better).

Which is why some philosophers of mind have reluctantly given up on physicalism (Chalmers, 2012), since it is beginning to look like the question is wrongly posed, specifically in the sense that we are trying to determine how buzzing neurons "create" the sound quale via efficient or material causation, when in fact, it simply may not work that way. Sound impressions, rather, may be properties of the *forms* of neural firing. Only when neurons are arranged and behave just so do they achieve the requisite form which has the property of an experienced sound quale.

Pain

Similarly, when pain fibers fire, due to stimulation by external events, we feel pain. But pain does not *derive* from pain fibers—it is not materially caused. Pain fibers can be isolated in petri dishes and stimulated all day long—but in such a case, nobody is feeling any pain. Only when embedded in an intact human being can they (under the right circumstances) *contribute* to the human consciousness feeling pain. But even then, human consciousness can complain of pain *even when there are no pain fibers at all* (i.e., phantom limb pain—when an amputee complains that the absent limb is hurting). In this case, the pain is associated with an entirely different set of neurons that are nevertheless achieving a similar form to that associated with an intact limb feeling pain. Thus, again, the conscious experience of the pain is something which obviously has *something* to do with pain fibers (usually), but cannot be attributed full causal power to the pain fibers themselves. The form can be achieved in multiple ways, and the experience transcends the fibers, but nevertheless contains them (sometimes!). This is not magic; this is merely the fact that integrated wholes possess properties over and above those possessed by the proper parts of those wholes, and the fact that quales are caused formally and not materially, though material is still needed. We are, after all, enmattered beings.

It is my contention, then, that *psyche* is a formally causal property—it is possessed by certain kinds of wholes. It is not a "substance" that is some-how different from matter. That would be a misplaced concrescence. Nor is psyche materially caused from matter, as we have seen. Psyche is, rather, a property of certain *forms* of bits of matter—which means arrangements, connections, and behaviors of those bits of matter *in relation to each other*. It is the relations that appear to make the difference, much more so than the bits.

Brain networks: parts within wholes that are parts within wholes, etc.

Neuroscience focuses and clarifies this analysis even further with respect to the particular type of psyche we label human conscious awareness. Compare the cerebellum to the frontal cortices. The cerebellum is a brain network that is involved with coordination of motor function and certain types of linear cognition. It is *not*, however, apparently needed to support the existence of consciousness. We know this because it can be removed without loss of consciousness. The *character and quality* of consciousness is certainly altered by doing this, of course, but consciousness continues to be observed. The frontal cortices, however, are another matter—if these are damaged or down-modulated with various chemical agents, consciousness disappears and the person becomes unconscious. But why is this? What's different about these two networks? The answer is *integratedness*. Where the frontal cortices are densely integrated, the cerebellum is not arranged in this manner; it is a largely "feed-forward" network that has inputs that it heavily processes and modifies before providing an organized output, with comparatively little in the way of feedback. Thus, neuroscience has given us clues as to the particular *kind* of form that is needed to possess higher levels of reflective awareness—integratedness.

And this integratedness varies across the brain and often contains many, many layers of integration (Freeman, 2000). For example, in the neutral state, the olfactory bulb typically displays a chaotic firing pattern that is not associated with any qualia. If enough olfactory neurons are stimulated, however, small networks begin to fire in a holistic manner that is self-sustaining and internally resonant. These networks then can begin to cohere with other resonating networks to make larger-scale resonating networks, on up several layers of expanding neural tissue, until there is large scale resonating firing that finally (after going through several processing stations) it makes its way to incorporating the frontal cortices, whereupon the person reports "smelling something". Each layer here possesses its share of psyche, and I believe *consciousness* obtains once the requisite amount of resonating networks obtain at a sufficient level of neural participation. This means the lower-order networks are likely associated with unconscious psyche in the manner Mills outlines.

Fragmented consciousness

The frontal cortices are themselves nearly self-contained units of conscious awareness that can function independently even if they are severed from one another via a corpus callosotomy—the so-called split brain state. In fact, split brain cases provide an interesting illustration to the point I'm trying to make: when not split (but still awake), a human has one "highest" center of conscious awareness and acts with a (mostly) coherent stream of singular experience. When the corpus callosum is cut, however, nearly all communication between the two frontal cortices is eliminated—thus the integratedness of the pair becomes drastically reduced. What remains, however, are two centers that are *themselves* still sufficiently integrated to possess the property of independent (slightly less) conscious centers of awareness, each controlling their connected body functions (the left brain controls the right body and vice-versa).

What's going on here? Weren't the left and right cortices still *there* before the callosotomy? Of course. But they were participating in the greater whole awareness before the operation, and so their own psyche began to participate in the larger network. That more comprehensive psyche was therefore "transcendent" of the individual cortices, in the sense that the property was present, even though the left and right cortices were there the whole time. The callosotomy just revealed that when decoupled, they were still capable of being centers of awareness on their own.

The more common cases of psyche fragmentation that we all observe in the consulting room are more subtle cases of the same phenomenon. Trauma, sleep deprivation, drugs, psychosis, or even simple fatigue can decouple a person from their normal state of relative integration, and this we observe as psychic fragmentation—the constellation of complexes or sub-personalities (in the case of severe trauma). What we strive for in therapy is a restoration of *integration*. Through therapy we strive to bring the disparate segments in harmony with one another, continually making connections between the patient's enantiodromias, *holding* rather than fleeing from the tensions of opposites. Through this painful process, greater levels of integration (i.e., more comprehensive integration of sub-units) are possible—what Jung called Individuation, i.e., becoming undivided. But this new state of un-dividedness that we strive toward is not "isolated" from the psychic frag-ments, aloof and alone in its unity. It is, rather, a property of the *form* that the parts are now participating in. The individuated ego (discussed here as an ideal end-point) is merely a person who is fully integrated in terms of all their interacting sub-personalities, intuitions, feelings, resentments, fears, hopes, etc. In the ideal case, these all work in harmony together *as one*, with all the parts working in an integrated manner as a holistic form which pos-sesses heightened awareness. In practice, of course, such integration must fend off the vicissitudes of life and all its fragmenting events and changing circumstances. Thus, the process goes on and on, with the chaos of life a centrifugal force that promotes fragmentation warring against the centrip-etal force of the transcendent function (with or without the amplifying help of a therapist) that strives toward integration.

This "one" unified psyche, however, is therefore only "transcendent" of the parts in the same way a property of a whole is transcendent of the parts—melody over notes, sound over auditory neural buzzings, "ouch" over firing pain fibers, etc. Individual neurons do not possess human con-sciousness themselves. Rather, they have *individual neuron consciousness*. But when arranged just so, they behave as a unit that does have human consciousness. Hence there is no contradiction in having a unified psyche that is transcendent of its parts while still containing their multiplicity—the objection to the Neoplatonic One is therefore, in my opinion, a misplaced concreteness on the One itself, treating it as if it were an object separated from the parts which compose it. Rather, the whole not only *contains* the parts but also has identity as a simplicity with its own unique properties derived from its form.

So where do the holistic properties come from?

Here is where the meat and potatoes of my argument act. We know from watching countless children develop from zygotes into full-grown humans that human consciousness "emerges" through the gradually increasing growth of an integrated brain and body system. But this emergence needs to be accounted for somehow. Both Mills and I are allergic to the idea that it simply appears *ex nihilo,* though there are some (Schaffer, 2017) who argue that this is just what happens—i.e., the emergence is *brute* emergence.

I argue that we can do far better than this, but the cost may be high depending on your temperament and tolerance for what might seem like a "zany" idea. But let me clarify: there are really only a few ways in which this emergence can be accounted for:

1   It doesn't occur because it's an illusion (eliminativism).
2   It occurs via brute emergence (epiphenomenalism, and some kinds of emergent physicalism).
3   It occurs via the coalescing of tiny psyches into macropsyches (micropsychism).
4   The holistic panpsychist argument I am defending.

I believe neither Mills nor I would place any hope in the first two. As I understand Mills' position, however, it is not clear to me how *precisely* he proposes psyche emerges in the developing human. I suspect he is deliberately avoiding precise mechanisms due to his phenomenological commitment— nothing wrong with that. Nevertheless, unless I misread him, he attributes to the universe what he calls a pervasive "pre-reflexive unconscious consciousness" (2021 p. 3). Though this might sound contradictory, it isn't— Mills is instead arguing that the universe has an omnipresent field of psychic potentiality, a kind of "fertile chaos" in which psyche can arise anywhere given the proper conditions. With greater and greater levels of complexity, then, we see the emergence of higher, more reflexive types of awareness— higher levels of psyche.

This position has a strong intuitive appeal to it—as we look inwardly and attempt to reconstruct how we got to where we are, this is indeed what it feels like. It is a type of panpsychism—the question is, are we dealing with micropsychism here? To answer that, we have to see how Mills describes the process of psychic emergence. On this, he says:

> I attempt to provide a framework where psyche emerges from the base material in which it finds its nascent self situated as embodied desire. In my system, psyche simply does not emerge *ex nihilo*, a point Goodwyn may have confounded, but is developmentally prepared through incremental forms of dialectical volution that organize into higher topographies of psyche evolution. The rudimentary given is already *a microprocess that matures into an organic mental whole we call mind or psyche*. Essence is diffused internally until it breaches externality, namely, the manifold of objects it encounters in consciousness (emphasis added).

This eloquent description of the process seems thoroughly reasonable. I cannot deny that it most likely happens in this way. My concern, however, comes in the italicized area. Why does one kind of material mass—say, a rock—which is also made of "psymatter" (an excellent term) *not* develop this sort of psyche but the organizing biomolecules that form a human body *does*? What's so special about us? Mills does not address this. We can press the question further here: neuroscience teaches us that there is a strong *regularity* to this process—cells that organize in integrated networks (even within an organism) behave as if they possess psyche (in varying degrees) like ours, whereas heaps of non-interacting bits of matter, like piles of sand, do not. But why?

Neither Mills nor I are saying that coalescing neural networks *cause* psyche to appear. We both agree psyche is already there. What separates our position is that Mills (if I read him right) proposes that the universe of psymatter has a pervasive set of micropsyches (his word) available which can, under certain conditions, mature into a whole which blossoms into a human psyche.

I believe, however, that this sort of panpsychism qualifies as micropsychism, because it proposes that isolated bits of psymatter—each possessing their own sorts of pre-reflexive or pre-reflective unconscious psyche—when arranged just-so somehow coalesce into a human being with a unified macropsyche which experiences qualia, melodies, sounds, pain, etc. This approach avoids the hard problem of neuroscience—namely explaining how buzzing molecules completely devoid of psyche can somehow create psyche. But it appears to have the combination problem—while it is true that *psyche itself* is not proposed by Mills to appear *ex nihilo*, nevertheless the macropsyche of such a system still does appear that way and must be accounted for. The observation running through all of my writing on this subject is simply to point out that when we do this, we are importing a mereological problem: we are attempting to explain the properties of the whole via the properties of the parts. I do not think this problem can be resolved without using brute emergence (see Jaegwon Kim, 2006, for further discussion). Since we are essentially asserting that the human macropsyche somehow develops simply because we are jamming a bunch of micropsyches together, we will encounter this problem, which has been in the conversation since William James at least (Chalmers, 2016). The underlying pluralism of the micropsychist proposal creates this issue. That is why I look to holism as a way around it. So unless Mills adopts *some* kind of holistic panpsychism, his analysis will require brute emergence. My observation is simply this: if we do not wish to accept brute emergence, we will have to claim with ancient and modern holists (Schaffer, 2010) that it *must be the other way around*.

Pluralisms and holisms have logical conclusions: in the pluralist universe, the properties of everything derive ultimately from physical simples (i.e., electrons, quarks, or whatever physicists discover). This viewpoint has been dominant since the days of Bertrand Russell. Prior to that, however, most philosophers were holists—the Neoplatonists among them. For them, the properties of everything on down to matter derive ultimately from the cosmos as a whole, and the tiny bits of matter upon which the pluralist places so much hope are considered not the most pluripotent, but the *least*: most derivative, most bereft of properties, most deficient in causal power. Mills calls this approach "backwards," but I must demur—it is only "backwards" given the *current* philosophical climate which is largely pluralist even when not explicitly stated as such. In any case, the holist approach proposes that properties of isolated parts derive from the wholes of which they participate when no longer isolated, on up to the most fundamentally real object: the whole known as the cosmos.

Schaffer (2010) provides an updated and much-cited defense of this ancient position, observing that there are a number of issues favoring holism, but most relevant here is the asymmetry of emergence. That is, we observe constantly that holistic properties emerge when isolated bits are arranged just so, but we never observe properties emerging when wholes are decoupled into isolated parts. The property of awareness acts in just this manner as well: when biomolecules are arranged just so, consciousness appears. When they are disintegrated (in a specific way), it disappears. Curiously, despite this defense, Schaffer (2017) refuses to part with physicalism, asserting that not only consciousness, but *all* properties of wholes must arise via brute emergence—each and every one. He does not seem perturbed by the explosion of brute emergences this requires. On that point, we part company.

In any case, when it comes to human consciousness, we know that only when *certain parts* are decoupled (i.e., frontal cortices, etc. as opposed to removing an arm) does consciousness disappear, which tells us that the property we are most interested in—consciousness—seems to only obtain in systems with a high degree of integratedness. Neuroscience also tells us that the degree of connectivity and integration are associated with higher, more coherent, and more coordinated and comprehensive consciousness (for more on integrated information theory, see Tononi, 2012).

From here to the cosmos?

It is here that I extrapolate the only logical conclusion: that progressively more inclusive, self-reflective, and expansive consciousness must correlate with greater and greater integration in a holistic system. Well and good, but this still doesn't explain *why* integration is the magic ingredient to produce consciousness. This is where the mereology comes in: this property—integratedness—is a property of wholes. Furthermore, it is a feature not of matter, but of the *form* of matter. Matter arranged in just such a way "obtains" human conscious awareness. So here, we are at last: where does this awareness come from?

Since I am a holist, I do not believe it derives from the parts. Why? Because it would mean I had to ascribe to ten thousand brute emergences—every time a system is arranged just so, macro-awareness just arrives brutely and without any way to explain it in principle—whether it emerges from the matter or whether it emerges from tiny bits of psymatter doesn't make any difference because the problem is the same: we are asking parts to conjure up properties of the whole. Hence, we must import some form of brute emergence to account for it. Brute facts are unavoidable; nevertheless, I prefer fewer of them. The only way to do this, then, is to say that consciousness appears in developing systems because they gradually approximate the one whole which possesses it maximally. In a human, this trades a trillion brute micro-emergences for one brute fact: that this maximally integrated whole has the property of maximally achievable consciousness. As a system approximates this maximally conscious form, it, too, begins to obtain a partial glimpse of the qualia that it must have. Why do I say "must" here? Because if the maximally conscious form—whatever it is—does not possess it, then we are back to brute micro-emergence again—the pluralist approach.

Rather, the qualia that arise in the system that approaches maximal integration (however distantly) get it *because* it is becoming more and more whole. But the priority of the whole is *ontological* priority—**not** *chronological*. This property is therefore not efficiently caused, it is formally caused. At this point, I can only imagine such a form to be the most integrated form possible. Such a form is—as it is a form—independent of time and space (just like attractor states in complex systems—see Goodwyn, 2013). This allows for the possibility that it could be merely a potential rather than directly observable at any given time. In any case, the one brute fact extant in this view is that that this maximally integrated form (whatever it is) must have the property of maximally conscious awareness and all qualia that anyone might experience. Hence everything we experience occurs because it participates in a tiny slice of the ultimate and most inclusive whole that is possible.

As such, though it is not required, the universe itself seems a good candidate for such a system, since it appears to be integrated at the quantum level as a whole, and, of course, there is nothing beyond it that might add to its integration since it contains all the matter that exists. Certainly, contemplating such a consciousness is vertigo-inducing. But that doesn't mean it is incorrect.

Mills asks, however: if this is so, how come we don't experience this cosmic consciousness? My answer is twofold. First, I would say that under normal conditions we might be like the humble neuron that receives inputs and sends outputs in accordance with its own internal intentionality that is nonetheless not aware or able to comprehend that it is a part of a system of 100 billion other neurons that compose a whole that itself has awareness. Why don't each of your individual neurons experience the quales that you do? The question therefore may simply be non-coherent, or at the very least, asking too much of humble neurons or (for that matter) humans. That said, however, my second answer is that there appear to be times when we actually do experience it, if we are to interpret such things as Near-Death Experiences or NDEs (van Lommel, 2011), the descriptions of mediums who claim to be channeling spirits (Carter, 2012), and those under other "mystical" states (Kelly & Kelly, 2009). Consistently one hears reports by subjects under such conditions of seemingly infinite consciousness, in which time is fluid and/or past and present are experienced simultaneously, the feeling of profound oneness, etc. This is *precisely* what an all-inclusive and prior consciousness would need to look like to do the causal work I am requiring it to do.

But then, why would such experiences be so coy? That is, why are they relatively rare? One answer is that the brain evolved to actually *limit* such ecstatic states (i.e., see Kastrup, 2014), i.e., the "filter" theory of panpsychism. Given that the brain has evolved greater and greater levels of integratedness, as the species neared higher and more expansive levels, it needed to, at the same time, evolve mechanisms which keep contact with the cosmic consciousness to a minimum in order to facilitate the survival of the species— after all, an organism which continuously experiences cosmic consciousness to a sufficient degree might not feel the need to bother taking care of its associated material body. Nevertheless, if this is so, there should be evidence that it "breaks through" every once in a while anyway, since such a biological constraint would inevitably be imperfect. This, of course, appears to be the case, particularly when entheogens, breathing exercises, deep meditative states, and the aforementioned near-death experiences appear to indicate (Kelly & Kelly, 2009).

Does all this amount, then, to a defense of the existence of God? I would say that depends on what you mean by "God". Cosmic consciousness might qualify or it might not—considering that such a consciousness would be (in my humble opinion) rather unlikely to be concerned with the sorts of things traditional religions seem to think God (or the gods) might be concerned with. Such a God would certainly be more akin to Spinoza's God than most others. Anyway, if it does, so what? Good for us, we finally have something tangible to hang on the concept of God, and a way to study it more rigorously, via the study of integrated systems. In any case, some cosmopsychists (for example, Goff, 2019), point out that cosmopsychism does not necessitate pantheism—it could be, the cosmic consciousness is simply a giant soup of qualia from which our qualia derive. I think this position has problems, but that's a subject for another day.

In any case, the way all this relates to Jungian psychology—outside of the fact that Jung himself had a near-death experience and described encounters with something akin to a cosmic consciousness—is simply this: the whole is greater than the sum of the parts. In other words, we are talking about expanding consciousness and improving harmony among the parts of a human psyche. This includes relatively more and relatively less conscious elements of the psyche. In the human mind, at least, it appears quite possible for parts to be highly conscious, and yet "one-sided" in Jung's terminology, in the sense that much that composes the person is being deliberately walled off or left out of the light. This is not a state of maximal integration.

Archetypes—a synthesis of views

Now we come full circle to the subject of archetypes. With these last thoughts, I will try to put together both of our approaches. Let's review what Mills (2018) observes about archetypes:

1   They are unconscious entities which are universal, self-propagating essences that generate subsequent psychic forms.
2   They direct and organize mental content.
3   Their products—the archetypal images—are multiple manifest in countless cultural expressions which nevertheless have universal origins.
4   They are the source from which phenomena manifest, conditioning all experience.
5   They exude and execute agency with independence and self-assertion— an "unconscious organizing principle that is internally impelled to materialize" (p. 212).
6   They have an internal *lack* that gives them agency to seek out ways to satisfy that lack—containing a "desire to wake, to apprehend itself, to manifest, is the expression of its own felt-being in relation to lack...the prototype of the human psyche" (p. 214).
7   They are encountered entirely from "within"—that is, within the human psyche alone.

Earlier in this discussion, I highlighted my concerns with this approach— namely, that I felt that however secure staying entirely within the field of human experience is, I did not feel we could completely escape the larger metaphysics of mind and matter when it came to finer details of psyche and archetype. But before we get into that, let me present *my* position on what archetypes are, and see how these two formulations compare, given all the work we have done on metaphysics.

In contrast to Mills' approach, I start with archetypal images (for full discussion, see Goodwyn, 2010, 2012, 2013, 2019, 2020a, 2020b, 2020c, 2022). Taking examples from the numerous cultural expressions from around the globe and throughout history, I note, with Jung, that there appear to be many examples of a given *type* whose structure does not change but whose various surface details appear to vary quite a lot. For example, there are many sun gods throughout the world, and whereas some of them are female, some male, some young, some old, etc., they all share certain fundamental characteristics that do not differ: all are deities associated with some or all of the following: knowledge, wisdom, sovereignty, fecundity, and civilization. There are no sun gods who embody fear, isolation, and death—at least none embodying death without subsequent ressurection. Similarly, nearly every culture studied has a variation on the "Beauty and the Beast" story, and oral variations on it date back thousands of years (Goodwyn, 2013).

Some theorists are skeptical that this observation has any real meaning—i.e., that such similarities are merely "abstractions" and do not represent the existence of any deeper structural "archetype as such" guiding their development (for example, see Colman, 2021). I feel there are some valid criticisms of Jung's choice to divide archetypes into archetypal image and archetype-as-such because in so doing, he invites a Kantian tangle of concepts that frankly just muddle the issue rather than clarify it. Nevertheless, I believe that (like so many things), Jung's intuition was on point even when his ability to describe what he was intuiting was sometimes lacking.

Thus, in my later works (Goodwyn, 2022), I restructure the archetypal image vs. archetype-as-such conceptual division and (I feel) put it on as precise and unambiguous footing as possible. Here's how it works—first I define what an archetypal image is, using Jung as a guide in all instances that it is possible, stating that an archetypal image is:

1   An *image and/or narrative.*
2   Symbolic, and only in the *indexical* sense,[1] and they must only symbolize *emotionally significant human experiences.*
3   Composed of inherited elements, but not be inherited themselves—i.e., we do not inherit images, although culturally-specific, learned content can be utilized in the construction of archetypal images.
4   *Resonant* (Goodwyn, 2013): i.e., so arresting that they are independently invented or repeated with high frequency across the globe.

Combining these criteria, an archetypal image is:

1   *An image/narrative that is an indexical symbol of an emotionally significant process that takes the subject's personal history, breaks it down and re-combines it into an expression conforming to innate organizational principles.*
2   *It is so easily arrived at that it has been independently invented frequently throughout history, despite large variations in background.*

This removes a considerable amount of grey area in terms of what is and what is not an archetypal image, eliminating a lot of what I see as conceptually sloppy work regarding archetypal images. For example:

1   Anything that is not a narrative or image is immediately ruled out. A cake recipe, for example, is not an archetypal image, nor are abstract

concepts like "number", "attachment", or "containment" (but, see below regarding archetypal elements).

2   A red octagon, even though it is an image and a symbol that means "stop", is not an *indexical* symbol—i.e., a symbol that "points to" something else—and so does not qualify. Likewise, if a snake image is simply used to represent snakes, it is not an indexical symbol and does not qualify either. In other words, only *symbols* rather than *signs* qualify.

3   Simple repeats of the subject's memories are not archetypes because they are not emotionally meaningful indexical *symbols* of one's lived experience.

4   A dream narrative, even when it is an emotionally meaningful indexical symbol of the dreamer's life, as most dreams are, does not qualify as an archetypal image unless it is organized in accordance with a sufficient amount of *archetypal elements* (discussed next). That is, it must conform to ordering principles derived from our impersonal embodied species history rather than personal history.

What remains is to elucidate what exactly the "innate organizing principles" of my italicized definition of the archetypal image are. In Goodwyn (2022), I propose that these principles should be called *archetypal elements*. Archetypal elements are then defined as *universally self-organizing, emotionally significant, embodied symbolic associations that partially compose an archetypal image*. This distinction replaces the "archetype-as-such" concept that corresponds to a given image. Rather than having a single (and very vaguely defined) archetype-as-such that is filled in by experience and one-to-one creates an image, the psyche inherits a *collection* of archetypal elements—akin to an "alphabet"—that it subsequently combines in different ways to construct archetypal images—akin to "words". These elements arise in everyone as a result of species-typical gene-environment co-action that *does not require* cultural instruction or observational learning. Rather, they are self-organizing in every biologically intact member of species *Homo sapiens* and can easily be verified via firmly established principles of developmental evolutionary biology.

Examples of archetypal elements include "cold = social isolation", "heat = intense emotion", "person = complex, seemingly intentful process", "light and dark = states of knowledge and safety", "the center = the aspect of greatest importance", "water = hostile unknown/mysterious", "water = life or meaningful feeling", "facial expressions and postures = emotional states", "size/up = powerful", "symmetry = conceptual harmony", "sphere/circle = wholeness", "objects = concepts/processes", and many others. These associations can be directly linked to our human biodevelopment and will reliably emerge even in individuals with severe deficits. They do not require cultural/observational learning and they are consequences of being members of species *homo sapiens*—i.e., they are innate. I justify the existence of all of these in Goodwyn (2022), and so won't belabor that here, but just to clarify with one example: "light = safety and knowledge" arises in us because we are diurnal mammals with acute visuospatially focused senses. It exists because we evolved from arboreal primates that needed precise depth perception that worked best during the day, and that need persisted due to our ancient species survival strategy of hunting and gathering. As such, it is inevitable that we will all develop an unconscious self-organizing symbolic association that links light with knowledge and safety and darkness with unease, the unknown, the unmanifest, etc. It does not take a unique poetic genius to invent this association and pass it on via cultural learning. Any human in any environment would develop this archetypal element on their own without any help, probably by age 7 at the latest, but likely much earlier.

This element can therefore find itself in all sorts of images, including sun gods, dark forests, the dark and light side of the Force, dark and stormy nights in pop-fiction, celestial cities of light, the darkness of the *prima materia* (where the darkness symbolizes "the unmanifest"), and so on, combining with the other elements in countless possible ways that are nevertheless latent in every human being. Using these archetypal elements, it becomes a fairly straightforward exercise to discern the meaning of various archetypal images that arise in therapy. Not only does my method provide a way of recognizing when one has emerged in the first place, it also guides the interpretation of it, provided the therapist avoids crass reductive errors and considers the patient/client's whole context.

Finally, I contend that the archetypal images do not emerge randomly, but at times of environmental stress that has *evolutionary* rather than merely personal significance. Like the individual raised in Hawaii who has never encountered cold weather, but then moves to Finland and finds herself shivering, some responses (i.e., the coordinated cold response) arise *due to our species history rather than our personal history*. Nothing in our example person's upbringing could have taught her to shift blood flow to internal organs, pull blood flow from the skin surface, and suddenly start shivering to produce heat. That response arises due to our *species* history. Archetypal images work the same way—faced with timeless environmental challenges, archetypal images arise to meet timeless human challenges and situations, only rather than focusing on temperature regulation, they focus on *psychic* regulation—producing expressions of meaning relevant to one's current social/intra-psychic environment that has nothing to do with personal history but instead arise from species history. The clinical example I give is that of an alchemical dream arising in a patient of mine who was just entering therapy (Goodwyn, 2022).

So, how does my theory measure up to Professor Mills' theory? Well, first, we must recognize that when Mills says "archetype", he is also redefining the archetype-as-such—i.e., the organization principles behind the "products" (#3 above). Therefore, we should compare his description of the archetype with my archetypal elements. I feel there is a great deal of agreement, provided we are careful about definitions. Archetypal elements, for example, are universal, self-propagating, and each contribute their own essence (essential meaning) to the images they compose, they can strongly direct mental content, and because they have firmly biological and evolutionary roots, they absolutely condition experience. Thus, there is strong agreement with the first 4 points of Mills' formulation with my own.

Then we can see that Mills goes into the preconditioning unconscious structures like I do, using a purely introspective analysis and the principle of sufficient reason, a method that adds depth and nuance by examining (as I see it) *what* processes link the elements together to generate the images, for what purpose, and at what time. For Mills, the deeper psychic process occurs when there is a noted *lack*, triggering a response that internally pushes itself to materialize—i.e., a sudden impulse, dream image, visionary experience, or what have you, that contains a preponderance of innate organizing principles. This internal force is so powerful it demands conscious attention and will utilize innate image-building principles in such a way as to be difficult to forget. Mills' insight adds a great deal of nuance and clarity here. Thus I cannot agree more, and my addition is that the *reason* for this power and force can be tied to the fact that it is an *evolutionary* response. In other words, all human genomes that did not have the ability to respond with archetypal images to timeless, frequently encountered but challenging situations have likely been eliminated long ago via natural selection. It is therefore part of our collection of potentials we inherit due to being members of *homo sapiens*.

Mills would need to confirm if this proposed synthesis works with his vision of what archetypes are, which leaves us with the last part of his definition—that archetypal images happen "entirely from within"—which brings us full circle. Presumably, this last qualification means "from within the individual psyche"—simple enough. But at this point, there exists a massive corpus of accumulated neuroscience. What are we supposed to do with it? Mills likely feels it is safest to bracket this question, and fair enough. But for me, ignoring it does not seem possible, since the data we have shows that there are pervasive regularities in correlations between our bodies and our lived psychic experience. This fact demands an explanation, and therefore demands a position on the mind–body problem, which means we must wade into the metaphysics of it.

Of the possible ways to connect neuroscience to phenomelogy, I chose holistic panpsychism, because it does not require brute emergence and requires only one brute fact: the existence of a maximal conscious form or cosmic consciousness (for simplicity, "CC" to represent these possibilities). We can apply this system to archetypes. Here, psychic experience is a property of integrated systems like human beings, however, it is not materially caused by the body, but is formally caused by being a proper part of the larger system of which *it* is a part, on up to the CC, the form from which all other properties derive. But, does this qualify as "within the human psyche"?

My answer: yes and no. The archetypal image *manifests* within the individual human psyche, but under this system the *boundary* of the human psyche, as separated from the larger CC, is not easily defined. When viewed entirely phenomenologically, one can only apprehend what presents itself to consciousness, which leads to backwards-engineering to determine what unconscious processes combined and developed to do so. Neuroscience teaches us that there are numerous centers of unconscious awareness that contribute to conscious awareness. We also know from everyday experience (i.e., sleep) that even when conscious awareness disappears, there remains many kinds of unconscious pre-reflexive awareness that continue. Moreover, clinical experience shows that even in cases of dissociative identity (Braude, 1995), there remains a deeper unconscious self that orchestrates conscious centers.

Under panpsychism, the source of all consciousness is the CC, and every part of the universe possesses a (relatively more or less decoupled) partial consciousness therein, with some local systems possessing it with a high degree in many layers of nested hierarchy (i.e., human consciousness as opposed to plant consciousness). In the human, this means fully awake, alert, and reflexive ("I am aware that I am aware") when in a highly integrated state, to many less integrated states (schizophrenia, trauma-induced fragmentation, drug use, neurological illness that disrupt connectivity, etc.), to being completely decoupled (i.e., death). What appears or disappears is, however, *local* consciousness. But since we are linking higher-order consciousness to higher levels of integration, by extension human consciousness—like the nested systems of the brain—can contribute to even higher orders of more inclusive transhuman systems. Thus, even if someone temporarily experiences CC through a transcendent vision or what have you, it is not correct to say "we" experience CC. Instead, we should say that CC may become temporarily partially manifest in our local corner of the universe centered on our body. Then, afterward, local consciousness resumes its more independent state. This might be analogous to a neuron temporarily experiencing human qualia for a moment and attributing it to *itself* afterward.

What all this means is that psyche shifts from less to more integrated and conscious states, even within a single individual, at times more and at times less inclusive or expansive, and nearly always in an extremely complex nested hierarchy. Thus, the question of whether or not something is within "the" psyche might be inadequate to handle the complexity of the situation. Which psyche? At what level? Containing what sub-systems? In any case, we still have an anchor point: *archetypal images.* These are experienced consciously by the individual psyche, but often with a sense of profound depth and comprehensive power. They are symbolic, emotional expressions that *transcend* the individual because they are composed of archetypal elements, and these elements are inherited and were crafted over millions of lifetimes of evolution. Again, such images do not *reduce* to genes—by themselves genes don't do anything, and crass reductions of this type are already ruled out by our holistic mereology anyway. Rather, archetypal images constellate when a particular life situation obtains, and they produce a set of behaviors in the brain and body that settles on the form needed to generate the archetypal image. But because the genes and environmental conditions—each with their own share of psyche as a sub-system—that coalesce into an archetypal image far exceed the mere spatiotemporal boundaries defined by an individual human, we cannot accurately say it occurs within an individual psyche, even though it is experienced within a single local field of consciousness associated with that body. Rather, that human body *itself* contains many copies of a genome that has a multi-million-year history. Hence the contribution it will have to the form of local, current consciousness will have echoes of that history within it.

This is perhaps why archetypal images present as "not me/far beyond me" and carry such numinous trappings as a result, speaking to us as if in the language of gods: in a very real sense they *are* expressions of a greatly transpersonal nature using a mode of expression eons older than the spoken word (narratives in images), the distilled experience of billions of human beings and other animals before. That this alone (even outside the precise meaning of the image itself) can heal a severely alienated ego should therefore not by surprising, since they are expressions that connect in a very tangible way to our greater, ongoing context. But the meanings also speak to timeless scenarios encountered by humans across the ages, and so can embody deep wisdom as well, provided we do not get too dazzled by them.

When Mills speaks of the blissful reconnection to source as a mere ego-driven wish-fulfilment, I can understand why: ego-driven wish-fulfilment does not have a great track record and it is an all-too-common occurrence. But then again, in the present paradigm, it seems there may be instances when it is not merely thus, but rather a genuine expression of (partial) CC breaking into an individual's awareness. And, if we can avoid bedazzlement as well as hasty dismissal, we can find a powerfully integrating peace that is nearly impossible to express in words, however fleeting.

Note

1 Indexical symbols are those which "point to" their meaning without explicitly representing it directly—i.e., footsteps in the sand point to the fact that someone has walked on the beach.

References

Braude, S.E. (1995). *First Person Plural*. Lanham, MD: Rowman & Littlefield.
Carter, C. (2012). *Science and the Afterlife Experience: Evidence for the Immortality of Consciousness*. New York: Inner Traditions.

Chalmers, D.J. (2012). Consciousness and its place in nature. In D.A. Chalmers (Ed.), *Philosophy of Mind: Classical and Contemporary Readings*. New York: Oxford University Press.

Chalmers, D.J. (2016). The combination problem for panpsychism. In D.A. Chalmers (Ed.), *Panpsychism* (pp. 179–215). Cambridge, MA: Oxford University Press.

Colman, W. (2021). *Act and Image: The Emergence of the Symbolic Imagination*. New Orleans, LA: Spring Journal Books.

d'Espagnat, B. (2006). *On Physics and Philosophy*. Princeton, NJ: Princeton UniversityPress.

Ficino, M. (2001). *Platonic Theology*. Cambridge, MA: Harvard University Press.

Freeman, W. (2000). *How Brains Make up their Minds*. New York: Columbia University Press.

Goff, P.. (2017). *Consciousness and fundamental reality*. Oxford: Oxford University Press.

Goodwyn, E. (2010). Approaching archetypes: Reconsidering innateness. *Journal of Analytical Psychology*, 55: 503–522.

Goodwyn, E. (2012). *The Neurobiology of the Gods: How the Brain Shapes the Recurrent Imagery of Myth and Dreams*. London: Routledge.

Goodwyn, E. (2013). Recurrent motifs as resonant attractor states in the narrative field: A testable model of archetype. *Journal of Analytical Psychology*, 58: 387–408.

Goodwyn, E. (2019). Comments on the 2018 IAAP conference on archetype theory: Defending a non-reductive biological approach. *Journal of Analytical Psychology*. 64(5):720–737. doi:10.1111/1468-5922.12543.

Goodwyn, E. (2020a). Archetypal origins: Biology vs. culture is a false dichotomy. *International Journal of Jungian Studies*, 13(2): 111–129.

Goodwyn, E. (2020b). Archetype: The contribution of individual psychology to recurrent symbolism. *Jungian Journal of Scholarly Studies*, 15(1): 5–19.

Goodwyn, E. (2020c). Archetypes and the 'impoverished genome' argument: Updates from neurogenetics. *Journal of Analytical Psychology*, 65(5): 911–931. doi:10.1111/1468-5922.12642.

Goodwyn, E. (2021). Bodies and minds, heaps and syllables. *Synthese*, 199:8831–8855. doi:10.1007/s11229-021-03184-7.

Goodwyn, E. (2022). Archetypes and clinical application: How the genome responds to experience. *Journal of Analytical Psychology*, 67(3):838–859.

Kastrup, B. (2014). *Why Materialism is Baloney*. Washington: Iff Books.

Keppler, J. and Shani, I. (2020). Cosmopsychism and consciousness research: a fresh view on the causal mechanisms of underlying phenomenal states. *Frontiers in Psychology*, 11: 371. doi:10.3389/fpsyg.2020.00371.

Kelly, E. and Kelly, E.W. (Eds). (2009). *Irreducible Mind*. Lanham, MD: Rowman & Littlefield.

Koons, R.C. and Bealer, G. (Eds). (2010). *The Waning of Materialism*. Oxford: Oxford University Press.

Kim, J. (2006). Emergence: Core ideas and issues. *Synthese*, 151: 547–559.

Mills, J. (2018). The essence of archetypes. *International Journal of Jungian Studies*, 10(3): 199–220.

Mills, J. (2022). Archetype, psyche, world: From experience to cosmopsychism. *International Journal of Jungian Studies*, 14: 1–20.

Schaffer, J. (2010). Monism: The priority of the whole. *Philosophical Review,* 119: 31–76.

Schaffer, J. (2017). The ground between the gaps. *Philosopher's Imprint,* 17(11): 1–26.

Shani, I. (2015). Cosmopsychism: A holistic approach to the metaphysics of experience. *Philosophical Papers,* 44(3): 389–437.

Sloman, S.A., Patterson, R., and Barbey, A.K. (2021). Cognitive neuroscience meets the community of knowledge. *Frontiers of Systems Neuroscience* 15: 675127. doi:10.3389/fnsys.2021.675127.

Tononi, G. (2012). Integrated information theory of consciousness: An updated account. *Archives Italiennes de Biologie,* 150: 56–90.

Van Lommel, P. (2011). *Consciousness Beyond Life: The Science of the Near-Death Experience.* New York: HarperOne Publishing.

Vazza, F. (2017). On the complexity and the information content of cosmic structures. *Monthly Notices of the Royal Astronomical Society,* 465(4): 4942–4855.

About the authors

Jon Mills, PsyD, PhD, ABPP, is a philosopher, psychoanalyst, and retired clinical psychologist. He is Honorary Professor, Department of Psychosocial and Psychoanalytic Studies, University of Essex, Colchester, UK; Faculty member in the Postgraduate Programs in Psychoanalysis & Psychotherapy, Gordon F. Derner School of Psychology, Adelphi University, NY and the New School for Existential Psychoanalysis, CA; and is Emeritus Professor of Psychology & Psychoanalysis, Adler Graduate Professional School, Toronto, Canada. Recipient of numerous awards for his scholarship including four Gradiva Awards, he is the author and/or editor of over 30 books in psychoanalysis, philosophy, psychology, and cultural studies including most recently *Psyche, Culture, World: Excursions in Existentialism and Psychoanalytic Philosophy*. In 2015 he was given the Otto Weininger Memorial Award for Lifetime Achievement by the Canadian Psychological Association.

Erik Goodwyn, MD, is Clinical Faculty at Eastern State Hospital, Clinical Associate Professor at the Billings Clinic, part of the WWAMI University of Washington School of Medicine—Billings, Montana affiliate, Department of Psychiatry, and Adjunct Professor at the University of Louisville, Department of Psychiatry. He has authored numerous publications in the field of consciousness studies, Jungian psychology, neuroscience, mythology, philosophy, anthropology, and the psychology of religion. He is co-Editor-in-Chief of the *International Journal of Jungian Studies*. His published books include: *The Neurobiology of the Gods: How the Brain Shapes the Recurrent Imagery of Myth and Dreams* (Routledge, 2012); *A Psychological Reading of the Anglo-Saxon Poem Beowulf: Understanding Everything as Story* (Mellen, 2014); *Healing Symbols in Psychotherapy: A Ritual Approach* (Routledge, 2016); *Magical Consciousness*, co-authored with anthropologist Susan Greenwood (Routledge, 2017); and *Understanding Dreams and Other Spontaneous Images: The Invisible Storyteller* (Routledge, 2018), which was a Finalist in the 2019 International Association for Jungian Studies Book Awards. He has delivered over sixty lectures, workshops, and presentations at conferences in the US, Switzerland, and Ireland.

Index

Note: Page numbers followed by "n" denote endnotes.

aboutness, as property of psyche 79
absolute interiority 10, 23–24n4
absolute negative interiority 24n4
Absolute Spirit 24n4
Ahbel-Rappe, Sara 109
alchemy dream 39–40
Alien archetype, as appearance of
    otherness 22
Anstoss (Fichte) 12, 97
aporias 1, 66, 106
aqua vitae 40
archaic ontology 1, 20, 46; appearance
    of 6–9; primordial instantiation of 11
arché 6, 23, 66
archetypal agency 47–48
archetypal elements 128–131
archetypal metaphysics: attractor states
    60–62; boundaries of explanation
    60–62; embodiment 59–60; ground
    essence 62–63; on holism 67–68;
    preliminary considerations toward
    63–67; psyworld 59–74; universal
    essence 62–63
archetypal theory of alterity 20–23
archetype-as-such 4; biology or culture
    30–32; and intermediacy 45–46
archetypes 6, 18, 113–132; alchemy
    dream 39–40; archaic ontology 6–9;
    archetypal theory of alterity 20–23;
    archetype debate 2–6; as autonomous
    8, 14, 16, 23n3, 48; as autonomous
    agents within mind 23n3; biology,
    innateness, and genes 29–30; biology
    vs. culture binary 30–32, 48–49; birth
    of 18–20; clinical example 39–40;
    contents in neither category 32–38;

defined 28; on essence 12–15; on form
    and appearance 11–12; implications
    for 38–39; as innate neuropsychic
    potential 4; inner constitution of
    9–15; metaphysics of difference 20–23;
    mythic example 39; parthenogenically
    born 8; and psyche 95–111; the sun
    god 39; synthesis of views 126–132;
    theory 38–39; as "transcendental
    entity" 23n2; as unconscious schemata
    15–18; on universality 10–11; and
    world 95–111
artificial intelligence (AI) 99
attractor states 60–62
autocratic, archetypes as 8, 48
autonomous: activity of the psyche
    71; archetypes as 8, 14, 16, 23n3, 48;
    character 17; ontological reality 103;
    quasi-autonomous units of experience
    10; teleological organization 100
axis mundi 35

"Beauty and the Beast" story 127
Beethoven, Ludwig van 87, 116
biblical *Genesis* 24n4
biology 30–32; and genes 29–30; and
    innateness 29–30
biology *vs.* culture binary 3, 30–32,
    48–49
biomolecules 81, 88, 115, 122–123
bioscience 79–83, 84–90, 107
bi-unity 15, 21
boundaries of explanation 60–62
brackets 79–83
brain networks 118–119
Brooke, Roger 68–70

Brooks, Robin McCoy 72
brute facts of psychic life 52, 56, 62, 79,
    86–87, 89–93, 102–105, 124, 130

callosotomy 119
Cartesian: demons 80; split 71
central nervous systems (CNS) 88
cognition 24n4, 106; complex spatial 33;
    linear 118
coherentism 62, 68, 78, 88, 113, 123
Collected Works (Jung) 2, 23n3
complex spatial cognition 33
consciousness: fragmented 119–120; and
    unconsciousness 113
corpus callosotomy 119
cosmic panpsychic process 67
cosmogonic act 20, 56, 95, 104
cosmopsyche 104, 105
cosmopsychism 88–89, 91, 95–111,
    116; plausibility 102–104; skepticism
    102–104
cosmopsychists 125
cosmos 110, 123–126
crypto-theology 110
culture 5, 9, 18, 20–21, 23, 30–32, 46–47,
    60, 62, 69, 110, 127

Darwin, Charles 4
d'Espagnat, B. 114
developmental monistic ontology 19, 63
Ding-an-sich 4, 45, 97
divinity principle 95, 104, 108
dream: alchemy 39–40; image 130;
    narrative 128

Ein Sof 107
Eliade, M. 7, 20
emanationism 3, 17
embodiment 59–60
*Encyclopaedia of the Philosophical
    Sciences* 24n4
Enneads (Plotinus) 108, 116
esse in anima 71–72
essence: ground 62–63; universal 62–63
"The Essence of Archetypes" (Mills)
    50–58; archetypal derivatives 54–55;
    archetype, characteristics of 51–52;
    archetypes, agency, and transpersonal
    52–53; explanations and boundaries
    of explanations 51; one/many 55–56;
    overview 50–51
existence: actual 19; autonomous 98; of
    consciousness 118; embodied 61, 98;

embodied physical 69; of God 109,
    125; material 65; mind independent
    17; naturalized form of 70; of other
    minds 80; physical 102; psyche as 72;
    psychic 62
experiences 95–111; individualistic 74n2;
    parapsychological 92; phenomenal
    78–79; primary 77–79; psyche as 72
explanandum 64
explanation, boundaries of 60–62
explicans 47
expression: aesthetic 18; cultural 52,
    126; emotional 131; facial 100;
    individualistic 74n2; mythic 39;
    quantitative 33; schematic 15–16;
    symbolic 33, 131; telic 15

fantasy: and reality 71; as reason 15;
    superstitious 57; and unconscious
    desire/defense/conflict 14
featureless absolute 11
"feed-forward" network 118
Ficino, Marsilio 87, 114
formless pervasiveness 11
fragmented consciousness 119–120
fundamental ontology 54, 62, 74n4,
    95, 104

Gallagher, S. 32
Geist 24n4
genes: and biology 29–30; and innateness
    29–30
genesis problem 6
Giegerich, Wolfgang 10; *The Soul's
    Logical Life* 23n4
godlike powers 53, 64
Goff, P. 78, 114, 125
Goodwyn, Erik 3, 5, 45, 49, 59, 69, 70,
    78, 95, 100, 107, 111, 129
ground essence 62–63

Hegel, G.W.F. 12, 15, 22, 23n1, 23n4, 71,
    99; Absolute 12; *Phenomenology of
    Spirit* 99; philosophy of Spirit 23n1;
    Science of Logic 23n4; *Wesenslogik*
    24n7
Heidegger, Martin 69, 74n4
Henderson, David 74n1
Higgs field 24n9
holism 67–68, 81
holistic panpsychism 91, 113;
    metaphysical realism into 113–114
holistic properties 120–123

Homo sapiens 128, 130
human psyche 9, 23n1, 29, 40, 54, 71,
    79, 87, 90, 92–93, 103–107, 110, 122,
    125–126, 131

immaterial entities 6
indexical symbols 132n1
individualistic experience and
    expression 74n2
innateness: and biology 29–30; and
    genes 29–30
integratedness 88, 118
integrated wholes 81, 114, 118
interconnectedness 55, 66, 105
intermediacy 45–46
internal infinity 10
internal ontology 63, 67, 70, 73, 77
intrapsychic Aristotelian
    foundationalism 52

James, William 122
Jones, Raya 4
Jung, C.G. 13, 22, 23n2, 28, 29, 41, 56,
    59, 74n1, 74n3; on archetypes 2, 5–6,
    8–10, 14, 16–17, 21, 28–31, 38, 42,
    48–49, 53–57; collective unconscious
    7, 68; *esse in anima* 71–72;
    Individuation 120; *Memories, Dreams,
    Reflections* 41; overarching question
    of psyche 110–111
jungian psychology 125

Kant, Immanuel 4; affinities 4; *Ding-
    an-sich* 4, 45, 97; *noumena* 12;
    phenomenal 60; tangle 83, 127
Keppler, J. 114
Knox, Jean 4, 28, 29

linear cognition 118
Lingnau, A. 33

macropsyche 89, 102, 115, 121–122
McMillan, Christian 71
Memories, Dreams, Reflections (Jung) 41
mentalized affectivity 99
Merchant, John 28
mesotheory of the third 46–47
messy epistemological burden 17, 53, 64
metaphysical baggage 108–110
metaphysical realism: into holistic
    panpsychism 113–114
metaphysics 23n4; archetypal theory of
    alterity 20–23; of difference 20–23

micropsyches 102, 105, 115, 122
micropsychism 86–92, 115, 117, 121–122
Mills, Jon 50, 77, 113, 126; *Origins: On
    the Genesis of Psychic Reality* 15, 74n4
mind-body problem 85–86, 101–102
minding matter 100–101
minding the mind 95–96
minds 99–100; minding 95–96
monistic ontologies 55, 63, 67
music 116–117
Myers, Steve 72
myth of modernity 4

natural 38; embodiment 73, 97–98; organic
    objects 98; selection 130; tendency 37,
    38; theology 109; world 69, 96, 99
naturalism 5
Naturalism *vs.* Supernaturalism debate 3
Naturphilosophie (Schelling and
    Hegel) 108
near-death experiences 90, 125
Neoplatonic 63; analogy 116; fashion
    110; holism 109; metaphysics 109, 110;
    Neoplatonic One 120; neutral monism
    63; principle 93, 107; worldview 115
Neoplatonic pole 66
Neoplatonism 114; and separateness of
    whole from its parts 115–116
Neoplatonists 93, 109, 123
noumena 12

ontological principle 96–98
ontology: archaic 1, 6–9, 11, 20, 46;
    fundamental 54, 62, 74n4, 95, 104;
    internal 63, 67, 70, 73, 77
onto-phenomenology 63, 65, 67–68, 72,
    87, 103, 111
*Origins: On the Genesis of Psychic
    Reality* (Mills) 15, 74n4

pain 117–118
pain fibers 86, 117–118, 120
Panksepp, Jaak 31
panpsychism 66, 85, 86–88, 102; holistic
    113–114
parapsychological: experiences 92;
    reports of visions 90
parthenogenically born archetypes 8
patternings 18, 22
phenomenal experience 78–79
phenomenological: discourse 5;
    encounter 71; experience 5; framework
    89; origins 52

Phenomenology of Spirit (Hegel) 99
philosophy of the One 108
physicalism 60, 85, 87, 89, 90, 92,
   101–102, 114, 117, 121, 123
Plato 7, 21
Platonic Forms 56
Platonic Ideal 12
plausibility and skepticism 102–104
Plotinus 108, 109; *Enneads* 108, 116
pluralism 88, 114, 122
pre-ontological 48
presence of essence 64
primary experience 77–79
psyche 4, 113–132; and archetype
   95–111; of bioscience 79–85; of
   brackets 79–83; cosmopsychism 88–89;
   emergence and brute facts 89–90;
   as existence 72; as experience 72; as
   higher unity 74; human 9, 23n1, 29, 40,
   54, 71, 79, 87, 90, 92–93, 103–107, 110,
   122, 125–126, 131; in Jung's system
   110–111; mind–body problem 85–86;
   origins of 77–93; overarching question
   of 110–111; overview 77; panpsychism
   86–88; phenomenal experience 78–79;
   primary experience 77–79; similarity of
   minds 81–83; and world 72, 73, 95–111
psychic activity 21, 56
"psychic entities" 23n2
psychic holism 105
psychic schemata 14
psychoanalytic schools 15
psychological experiences 31
psychology 23–24n4; analytical 38, 46,
   110–111; developmental 3, 28, 32;
   empirical 2; evolutionary 5; human 71;
   Jungian 125; naturalized 111; of place
   69; social 3; transpersonal 66
psymatter 105–107, 122, 124
psyworld 59, 68–73; archetypal
   metaphysics and 68–73; *esse in anima*
   71–72; psyche and world 73; psyche
   as existence 72; psyche as experience
   72; psyche creates world 72; world as
   psyche 73
pure knowing 23–24n4

Rationalism *vs.* Empiricism debate 3
realism 98; metaphysical 113–114
reductive scientific naturalism 98
resonant attractors 5

Roesler, Christian 4, 29, 41
Russell, Bertrand 122

Saunders, P. 28
Schaffer, J. 123
schemata: psychic 14; unconscious
   1, 15–18, 46, 53, 61, 96, 101;
   variegated 10
Science of Logic (Hegel) 23n4
scientific naturalism, reductive 98
Segal, Robert 6
self-generated learning 34
Shani, I. 114
Skar, P. 28
skepticism and plausibility 102–104
The Soul's Logical Life (Giegerich) 23n4
sound 117
Spinoza, Baruch 125
Spirit 23n1, 24n4, 65
split brain state 119
statue of Zeus 88, 116
Stevens, Anthony 3, 4, 31
the sun god 39
supernatural 74n2; macroanthropos
   17, 53
supervenience 3, 17, 66

transcendental heavens 105–107
transpersonal: archetypes 17, 53; defined
   74n2; frameworks 65; psychology 66;
   reality 5; supervenience 66

unconscious/unconsciousness 23n1; and
   conscious 113 schemata 1, 15–18, 46,
   53, 61, 96, 101; self-consciousness 19
universal essence 62–63
universality: archetype 10–11; within
   difference 21; self-enclosed 18; shared
   110; subjective 99, 111
unus mundus 23n2, 24n4, 63

variegated schemata 10
Vazza, F. 114

Whitehead, A.N. 22, 106–107
world 113–132; and archetype 95–111;
   and psyche 95–111; as psyche 73;
   psyche as 73; psyche creating 72;
   psyche not in 73

zeitgeist 114

For Product Safety Concerns and Information please contact our EU
representative GPSR@taylorandfrancis.com
Taylor & Francis Verlag GmbH, Kaufingerstraße 24, 80331 München, Germany

www.ingramcontent.com/pod-product-compliance
Lightning Source LLC
Chambersburg PA
CBHW050613280326
41932CB00016B/3031